The Other Side of
Notting Hill

The Other Side of
Notting Hill

From Wartime to the Westway

Roger Rogowski

Foreword by ALAN JOHNSON

For my parents, Eileen (1921–1977) and Jan (1924–1986).
Their decision to move to Kensal Road in 1952
ultimately led to this book being written.

Front cover photo © The Royal Borough of Kensington and Chelsea; back cover
photo © Roger Rogowski

First published 2018

The History Press
The Mill, Brimscombe Port
Stroud, Gloucestershire, GL5 2QG
www.thehistorypress.co.uk

British Library Cataloguing in Publication Data.
A catalogue record for this book is available from the British Library.

ISBN 978 0 7509 8906 0

Typesetting and origination by The History Press
Printed and bound in Great Britain by TJ International Ltd

Contents

Foreword

North Kensington has for too long existed in the shadow of its more prosperous neighbour, Notting Hill – the proud possessor of a film title and even a political 'set'. We didn't see much of Julia Roberts or Hugh Grant on the mean streets of London W10, although as contributors to this book recall, plenty of gritty TV dramas such as *Z Cars* used North Kensington as a backdrop. Its streets and alleys, pubs and bookies, totters and prostitutes were certainly well-known to the real coppers; the ones who only dared patrol in threes through streets such as Southam Street from the mid-nineteenth century onwards.

As somebody once said, nothing is more responsible for the good old days than a bad memory. This book doesn't gloss over the crime, the violence or the squalor. Its contributors are, I suspect (having never had the pleasure of meeting them), among the vast majority of W10 residents who were decent law-abiding citizens battling against the odds to carve out a better life. I recall arriving in Ruston Close, off St Marks Road, early on Saturday mornings as I helped Johnny Carter with his milk round to see every other doorstep being scrubbed and whitened by turban-headed women on their hands and knees. It was as if they were trying to scrub away the terrible history of that cul-de-sac, previously named Rillington Place, and the horrific murders that took place at the house in the corner – No. 10.

For us younger residents of North Kensington in the 1950s, the future was bright. We grew up in an age of social mobility where jobs were available, educational opportunities were expanding and horizons that previously seemed distant, moved ever closer. Our parents had been through enormous deprivation and the horrors of war, whilst we witnessed a new post-war settlement that changed our landscape so rapidly, albeit damaging close-knit communities and a settled way of life in the process. Had Charles Dickens walked down gas-lit Southam Street in 1950, the year I was born, he would have been entirely familiar with the housing conditions. By the mid-1960s the slums had gone – in their place, tower blocks.

This book illuminates a London that has vanished. It is an important contribution to the social history of the unmajestic end of the Royal Borough.

Alan Johnson, 2018

About the Author

Roger Rogowski was born and spent his childhood in Notting Hill from 1953 to 1966. He has written several articles and blogs on local history and led or supported several local history projects. Inspiration for this book came from leading classes and discussion groups at his old primary school in North Kensington as part of a school project. Not only the children but also the teachers were fascinated by stories about the area as it was. A call was put out on social media and, just over a year later, more than thirty people contributed their memories or photographs for the book.

Acknowledgements

This book would not have been possible without the wonderful people who gave their time to share their memories so I'm very grateful to Margaret Burdsey, Pauline Clark, Babs Coker, Brian Collins, Mossy Condon, Bob Crawley, Vee Davis, Ken Farrow, Derek Ford, Frank Hale, Ray Matthews, Susan Mcmahon, Gwen Nelson, Alan Peverall, Charlie Phillips, Marg Pithers, Maureen Rafferty, Barbara Reynolds, Jeannie Rowe, Richard Rowlands, Jean Russell, Christine Smith, Dennis Smith, Margaret Stedman, Reg Thackeray, Jane Traies, John Traies, and Alan Warner. (Sadly, Jean Russell died before this book was published. Jean was an engaging storyteller and had a great memory – she told me far more stories about her life and family than I was able to included here.)

Thanks also go to everyone who copied or sent me a huge number of old personal photographs, even though I was only able to use a small proportion of them in this book. Credits for the photographs in this book are listed on page 10.

Thanks also to local historian Tom Vague, who provided me with the transcript of his interview with Vee Davis; to friend and former W10 neighbour Gwen Nelson; authors James Collins, Janet Davies and Terry Hope; local historians Dave Hucker, Sue Snyder, Maggie Tyler; librarian Dave Walker, who provided valuable advice and/or practical support along the way. Thanks to my wife, Chrissie, for acting as occasional sounding board and for putting up with my obsession with this project, especially in the final few months.

Final thanks go to former Southam Street resident, politician and author of *This Boy* Alan Johnson, who wrote the Foreword.

Picture Credits

Copyright is held by the following for images in this book:
Alamy: page 20
Pauline Clark: page 182 (bottom)
Babs Coker: page 33
Bob Crawley: page 51
Derek Ford: page 111
Christine Kelliher: pages 52 and 182 (top)
Museum of London: pages 93 and 94
Ray Matthews: page 21
Mirrorpix: page 194
Krys Mozdzynski: page 112
Gwen Nelson: page 160
Roger Rogowski: page 68
Royal Borough of Kensington and Chelsea: pages 69, 133, 205 and 206
Jean Russell: page 34
Lynne Shipton: page 193
Margaret Stedman: page 144
Helen Tilley: page 159
Jane Traies: page 134 and 145

Introduction

Postal sub-districts were introduced in 1917, designating North Kensington as W10 and its more famous neighbour, Notting Hill, as W11, but the idea that Notting Hill stretches into W10 isn't a modern invention by hopeful estate agents. When the oldest underground railway in the world was extended from Paddington to Hammersmith in 1864, the station we now know as Ladbroke Grove was originally named Notting Hill. Nearly a century later, in 1958, the violent inter-racial disorder that broke out in the streets in the north of the borough was dubbed the Notting Hill riots and the murder of Kelso Cochrane in Southam Street in 1959 was referred to as having taken place in Notting Hill by the national media.

When the urban landscape that we see now was developed from farmland, predominantly for middle-class families, North Kensington almost immediately underwent rapid change. The houses mostly lacked the leafy squares, were too small and too close to the railway and the canal to appeal to their intended market, and the increasingly desperate developers started to offer many of the houses for multiple occupancy by the working class. As that happened, houses that were built later were even smaller and out went the ornate external and internal decoration added to earlier buildings in order to maximise the developers' return on their investment.

As a result, North Kensington became a firmly working-class area and, because houses and flats were relatively cheap to rent, immigrants were also attracted to the area, starting with Irish navvies and their families and Jews fleeing persecution in Eastern Europe. Many of the streets of Notting Hill closest to North Kensington also started to be occupied by the working class as the first immigrants were followed, over the next hundred years, by people from Spain, Italy, Poland, Cyprus, the West Indies, Portugal, Morocco and other countries.

Architecturally, there was very little to distinguish the houses in either area, even if the houses in the north often looked like smaller and cheaper imitations of the ones to the south, where the houses were well maintained with orderly gardens and almost always occupied by single middle-class families. To the north, the houses were generally run-down and almost always occupied by the working class. From soon after the area was developed in the nineteenth century even up to around the 1970s, Notting Hill and North Kensington were more or less defined by Booth's 'poverty maps', which were published in 1889 and 1898/9. The difference between the two areas was and still is therefore less about a defined border and more about the relative affluence of who lived where, and that boundary has been creeping further north as gentrification or regeneration, depending on your point of view, has claimed more and more streets.

In common with urban and rural communities across the country before large-scale centralised manufacturing and supply chains were developed in the late twentieth century, North Kensington and working-class Notting Hill was self-sufficient in many respects. Most people both lived and worked locally. Skilled and unskilled jobs were plentiful and there were always other opportunities to earn money. Even if the rewards were small and the work was hard, there was a thriving grey economy operating on a cash-in-hand basis. It was well known that it was possible to walk out of a job one day and into another one the next.

Often, people were born, grew up and started families locally, so it was common for other family members to live nearby or even in the same house. Living conditions were almost always cramped in a way that probably can't be imagined today. Multiple families sharing houses built for single families, sometimes living and sleeping in one or two rooms, was the norm and a large part of life was played out in the street when people had little in the way of home entertainment. It would be a mistake to think that it was an entirely poor area though. Most shop owners lived on the premises above their shops and, as small business owners, they were relatively comfortably off, and many skilled and clerical workers lived in the area. Likewise, although the area was associated with appalling slums, most people who lived there at the time would baulk at the word. They were people's homes and the large majority kept their homes and themselves as clean and 'presentable', to use a word my mum used a lot, as their resources allowed. Very few people lived in what might be considered squalor and, even if they did, it was because they had no choice.

Housekeeping was almost a full-time job, even if a lack of money meant that many women went out to work or did home work. Even in the 1960s, very few families in the area had any of the household appliances that we take for granted today and very few people owned a car, so shopping was done on an almost daily basis in local shops, and washing was done by hand either at home, at the local baths or taken to the local bagwash.

All of this meant that people got to know who lived around them more readily and urban areas such as Notting Dale and Kensal Town were recognisable communities to an extent that is almost unknown in cities and large towns today. The breakdown of the culture of close-knit communities has been a slow process driven by a number of factors over many decades but that change occurred more quickly, almost brutally, in many urban areas across the country as part of the post-war slum clearance programme. In North Kensington, as elsewhere, local communities were broken up by slum clearance but also by the building of the Westway in the mid-1960s. At the same time, almost simultaneous with the start of the Notting Hill Carnival, Portobello Road became a trendy place to visit and local pubs and clubs became part of the Sixties scene. The area wasn't far from central London but it was cheap and it suited the emerging alternative lifestyles of the time.

Where the original Victorian houses still remain today, many have been converted back to single occupancy and upmarket shops have appeared along Golborne Road and the bottom of Portobello Road and other shopping streets. Houses that escaped demolition now change hands for millions and the shops and businesses that surround them are meeting the needs of the people who own them. The area is almost unrecognisable from the one that we would have seen walking around anytime from the 1860s to the early 1960s.

Golborne and Portobello Roads as traditional high streets, with their bakers, butchers, greengrocers, chemists, clothes and hardware shops, are long gone as they are almost everywhere, but what will strike anyone who remembers the area as it was is the quietness of the surrounding streets. Because it was a place where people worked as well as lived, housewives shopped every day and children played in the streets in almost all weathers, even side streets were never as deserted as they appear today. The area as it was only exists now in the memories of people who lived there at the time. Those times have already been described in excellent books such as Alan

Johnson's *This Boy*, Mark Olden's *Murder in Notting Hill* and Julie Ryan's *In and Out of the Lion's Den*. I recommend reading them all but it seemed to me that old North Kensington and working-class Notting Hill needed another book that provides a more comprehensive description of those times, told by as many people as possible who lived through those times.

The way that people lived there up until about the early 1960s would be almost unrecognisable today, and I should know. Born in 1953 in Kensal Road, I moved out in 1966 when almost all of the immediate area between Golborne and Great Western Roads, the canal and the railway, was demolished to make way for Trellick Tower. There was no reason to go back and life got in the way, so I didn't return for almost fifty years, when I went really only because I was close by with about an hour to spare on a December afternoon in 2014. All but about a dozen of the old Victorian buildings between the canal and the railway in Kensal Town had gone and likewise the buildings either side of Golborne Road between the railway and the bottom end of Portobello Road were almost like façades, with modern housing in the streets leading off them.

Since that first re-acquaintance with North Kensington in 2014, one thing led to another and I've met up again with many of my old school friends and met many new friends who remember the area from those times, who were happy to share their stories. Because all of those stories have been drawn from living memory, I have only been able to go back as far as the Second World War, while I've chosen to end the narrative at about the point that the area started to undergo the major changes in the mid-1960s that I've already described. I was able to issue invitations to take part via social media to almost 4,500 people. Almost all of them could probably have told similar stories but the people who did, have evoked those times very well, even though we are all describing events that took place more than fifty years ago during our childhood or early adulthood. I've also contributed my own memories. Checking on a map, everyone featured in this book lived within a mile radius and all but three lived within a half-mile radius of each other.

I transcribed, as closely as possible, what was said, apart from some editing for continuity and where places, events and dates could be checked and needed correcting. In using the exact words they used, I hope I've also captured the diversity of the area as it was. Although I had a list of set questions to ask those that I interviewed, most took the first few questions as a prompt and spoke in the order that their memories came back to them, so there was quite a lot of re-ordering to be done to get the material into the relevant chapters.

Something will almost certainly occur to you as it did to me about midway through the project. Even though the group effectively selected itself – those who were happy to take part – it didn't meet my expectation in representing what I think of as the diverse racial and cultural nature of the area but, on reflection, I realised I was looking at the area from the perspective of the area as it became later and is now. Check almost any photograph of a crowd or group of people in North Kensington from, say, the 1950s – and there are plenty of them thanks to photographers like Roger Mayne, Ken Russell and Corry Bevington – and the faces staring back don't represent the ethnic profile that we'd see today. Even if I only have anecdotal evidence and my instincts, the group of contributors is about as representative as it can be of the area at the time.

How best to arrange the stories took some thought and, in the end, after some wise advice, I decided to order them by theme rather than devote a chapter to each contributor and, within those themed chapters, each of the contributor's stories is arranged chronologically. In this way, the narrative provides a more rounded picture of different aspects of old North Kensington life, like work, shopping, play and so on, and it's almost as if twenty-nine people are in a room having a discussion.

The first chapter, In the Beginning, looks at how the people I met and their families came to live in the area. Although the area was already well established, having been developed rapidly in the nineteenth century, a large number of people seem to have moved into the area or even arrived in the country only a generation before, reflecting its transient nature. In Chapter 2, Our House, people describe what their homes were like. Most of us used to say 'our house' but almost everyone lived in a flat, mostly in a terraced house converted for multiple occupancy. Although some purpose-built blocks had already been constructed before the war, they were few and far between.

In Chapter 3, Home Life, people describe how they spent their time at home and what it was like to live there. Outside or shared lavatories were common and purpose-built bathrooms were rare. Bedrooms were almost always shared, often by the whole family. In Chapter 4, Down our Street, people describe their immediate area, the local landmarks and how people in the immediate neighbourhood interacted, and in Chapter 5, Boys and Girls Come out to Play, looks at how and where they socialised as children at a time when children learned to become relatively independent and 'streetwise' at an early age, spending much more time outside without parental guidance than would be considered acceptable today.

Chapter 6, Schooldays, obviously looks at local school life, which will seem very different to younger generations. Chapter 7, Shopping, looks at how that activity was influenced by the lack of car ownership and the presence of small independent shops. As well as Golborne and Portobello Roads and the markets, which provided almost everything anyone would need, when a street corner wasn't occupied by a pub, it was usually occupied by a corner shop, so people almost always shopped within walking distance of home.

The adult world is described in Chapters 8 and 9, Work life and Social life. Work was plentiful in the local area, but money was often tight so, often, housewives worked as well. The work ethic was strong and picked up at an early age, and many were quite inventive and independent in earning some pocket money, either formally in after-school or Saturday jobs or informally in a variety of cash-in-hand enterprises, even if they weren't always strictly legal. Social life for adults more often than not meant the local pub or social club, a visit to one of the local cinemas or inviting family and friends round for a party. Formal eating out was almost unknown, unless it was some form of celebration, and even then it was beyond most people's means.

Likewise, holidays as we know them today, were almost completely out of the question for working-class families but many still found the opportunity to have a change of scenery at least for a few days or a week during the year. Chapter 10, Holidays, looks at how people spent their time away.

The period covered in this book was hugely eventful, starting with the Blitz and, in the post-war period, the Notting Hill riots, the murder of Kelso Cochrane, and the 1959 general election in which Oswald Mosley stood as a local candidate. All of them made headline news. Part of the Profumo affair was played out in the area and Portobello Road was starting to become part of the Swinging Sixties with numerous films and television programmes being shot on location in the surrounding streets. Chapter 11, Headline News, looks at what people remember about those and other events. Finally, either as a result of slum clearance or out of choice, many people left the area. By then, the area was undergoing rapid change and Chapter 12, All Change, looks at how that changed their lives.

There is a wealth of first-hand accounts here that speak about life in the mid-twentieth century that contrasts hugely with the way we live our lives more than half a century on. Very few contributors expressed any opinion about which parts of life were better or worse and, to be fair, I tried to steer everyone to simply recall what life was like back then. In the main, I've tried to avoid any analysis of how we lived and I leave you to form your own opinions about how life has changed over the years. For younger readers, I imagine L.P. Hartley's quote that 'the past is a foreign country' must seem very true. As well as the 'official' themes denoted by the chapter headings, you will probably see other themes running through the narrative, stories about difficult living conditions, neighbourliness, generosity, humour, love, racism, tragedy, criminality, violence and even the mundanity of everyday life. If any of it seems surprising or shocking or anything else, well, that's the way it was. There is a third dimension to this book, too, as readers can follow the stories of each of the twenty-nine contributors' lives.

I've been privileged to meet some wonderful people who have been happy to share their memories. I enjoyed listening to their stories and I hope you find them as enjoyable. In undertaking this project, I've also learned a lot about the area as it was that I didn't know. As I had to, I've read the text through several times but the ability of the narrative to bring back to life the area in that period up to the mid-1960s hasn't diminished for me with each reading. Whether you remember the area from those times or whether you are new to the topic, I hope it does the same for you.

Roger Rogowski, 2018

one

In the Beginning

∽ Frank Hale:

My parents, Reuben and May, were born in Notting Hill and so was my grandad. My grandad, James Hale, was one of several kids. When he finished school, there was no work for him in the area so he cycled all the way out to Letchmore Heath to get a job and ended up lodging at a Mrs Stone's house in the village.

I was born in Westbourne Park Road in 1938. Our house was opposite the entrance to Elgin Mews about ten houses up from the convent that used to be on the corner of Ladbroke Grove. It was called Cornwall Crescent then. We lived at No. 197. Later on, the road was renamed and the houses were renumbered, so the house became 341 Westbourne Park Road.

❋ Jean Russell (née Hemming):

I was born in our front room in Beethoven Street. My mum's mum, Granny Warner, lived in our street with two more aunties and another one next door and Auntie Hazel lived upstairs from us, so that was five sisters, and my mum's brother lived a few doors from us. One more sister lived in Quex Road in Kilburn, so we were surrounded by caring aunties and our gran. My grandad died when I was young.

🖤 Ken Farrow:

My mum married in 1938 and had seven kids. We lived at 48 Hazlewood Crescent in 1948. Before that, we lived in Kilburn Lane but I don't know much about that. We had the ground floor and the basement in Hazlewood. There was me, two brothers, one sister, my mother and my grandmother.

My dad died in 1949. He was a Canadian serviceman. We moved to Golborne Gardens in 1953. In 1956, my mum met my stepfather, remarried and moved into his house at 82 Kensal Road. My mum worked in Clark's pet shop opposite his house, so I suppose that's how they met. He had four sons and daughters from his first wife. One of them was married by the time we moved in, so there was him and his three children, me, my mother, grandmother, three sisters and two brothers. My stepfather was born in 1901 and served in the First World War. He rose to the rank of sergeant major. My sisters thought he was a bit of a tyrant at home but he was only doing what he thought was right.

The newly completed section of Ladbroke Grove between Lancaster Road and the railway bridge, 1866. The extension from Paddington to Hammersmith was opened in 1863 and construction on the surrounding farmland started soon after. Apart from two lamp posts, the land on the other side of the bridge looks undeveloped.

Stebbing Street children's tea party to celebrate King George V's Silver Jubilee, May 1935. Stebbing Street was demolished in the mid-1960s and is now occupied by Norland North Open Space Park.

Jane Traies:

Our grandmother, Reenie Taverner, was from an Irish family who moved into the area during the Irish migration, probably two or three generations before her. Reenie's family name was Bryant. She grew up in Notting Hill and, like so many working-class girls at the time, Reenie went into service as a maid in a big house. She worked for Sir Charles and Lady Oliphant in Leinster Gardens, then she moved to More Place in Betchworth, then she went to Betchworth Manor, then Deep Dene in Dorking for two years and then Sand Hills in Betchworth.

Our grandad Jack Taverner's family came from Surrey. He grew up in Bagshot. Reenie and Jack met when they were in service together before the First World War. Like most old soldiers, Jack stopped short of describing his war experiences but our dad told us much later that Jack was a gunner in the Royal Field Artillery and that, after the war, he used to go with him to some of his reunions, which were usually held at the Putney Constitutional Club. The only story the rest of us ever heard was about the day in Palestine when Jack was tending his horses and a soldier ran up and said, 'Sergeant Taverner, the war's over!'

When he came back from the war, Jack and Reenie got married. The first two or three years of their marriage, they kept a pub in Surrey. I think they moved to Golborne Road and opened their shop in about 1920 because our mum was born in 1919 in Surrey and our auntie and uncle were born later in Golborne Road. Jack never lost his love of horses and you can imagine his delight when the King's Troop came past his shop from their barracks at St John's Wood and sometimes had to stop by the shop and wait to cross Ladbroke Grove on the way to Wormwood Scrubs. Reenie had two brothers who were both single men who lived with Grandad and Grandma. We've traced our dad's family, the Traies, as far back as the 1891 census in Elgin Crescent. Our mum and dad got married in St John's Church on the hill. They lived in Elgin Crescent then.

🌿 *Pauline Clark (née Harding):*

My grandparents lived in Southern Row. My grandfather was a greengrocer and my grandmother worked in a laundry as an ironer. They had six children and they all married and moved away except my mother. My father lodged with them and ended up marrying my mother. My father was born in 1897 and my mother in 1907. Father was an orphan. He had lost his parents and brothers in the First World War. When they got married, my parents moved to 10 Bosworth Road, which was the mission house.

I am the youngest of six children. We occupied the top two floors in the mission house as the mission held meetings on the ground floor. The mission moved down the road next to the rec, so we still had Girls' and Boys' Brigade and Sunday school. Later, the mission was sold to Addison Electric Company. My parents cleaned the company premises to help with the rent. Mum would clean the offices and Dad would clean the factory. I would help cleaning bins and ashtrays starting at 8 years old. By the time I was 10, I was sweeping and washing floors.

🐚 Derek Ford:

My mum, Maud Day, was born in 1918 at 2 Silchester Terrace where my nan and grandad still lived so I was always down that end visiting them and going to Lancaster Road Baths. My mother's family owned the house, which was very unusual for the area then. My mum and dad married in 1939 and went to live at 49 Silchester Road, and then moved to Chesterton Road. I was born in 1947 in Chesterton Road, a few doors along from the Percy.

🦋 Alan Warner:

I was born at No. 4 Beethoven Street between nine o'clock and a quarter past nine on 10 December 1947. I was the fourth child of Kate and Bert Warner. By the late Fifties, there were nine children: five sisters and three brothers. I vividly remember visiting Nan one night and sitting with the lights off watching a roaring coal fire and trying to see shapes in the flames. She was a lovely gentle lady who was loved but sometimes bullied by Grandad Warner, who was an RSM [regimental sergeant major] in the Black Watch Regiment. My father was in the Royal Fusiliers and was for a time during the Second World War stationed at the Tower of London as well as serving in North Africa.

🍀 Richard Rowlands:

My dad came from Wales in 1936 and moved down by the Prince in Middle Row. It was next door to a scrapyard. Corky used to own the scrapyard. They called my dad Taffy. He had six years in the war. He was a hard man. My two brothers had murders with him because he was regimental. That was the way he was. My mum come from over the Avenues. Her mum lived in Third Avenue. I can still see my old nan because they were all the same in a pinny and National Health glasses. Everyone loves their nan.

Gwen Nelson (née Martin):

We – myself and my parents, Victor and Gerry Martin – moved to Golborne Road from Lambeth in 1952. After returning from being a POW in Lamsdorf and being demobbed, Dad never settled into a job, working for a few weeks here and there as a spray painter, window cleaner, anything unskilled that was going. Mum always told of how Dad would come home, say he'd chucked in his job and hand her his final pay packet. She would go out, spend all of it and then tell him they had no money so he'd better find another job in a hurry.

In Lambeth, we lived with my grandparents, Alice and Frederick Ireland. Grandad Ireland was a master builder. By coincidence, my great-grandfather Thomas Ireland built and owned Nos 51–6, 66–72 and 74–8 Golborne Road, all of which are still standing. Nana would look after me while Mum worked part-time on the till at Lyons or ABC teahouses. Mum would also take in piecework sewing elastic into children's swimsuits at three farthings a garment.

Before the war, Dad worked as a bacon hand for Frost's, an early supermarket group. One day he confessed to Mum that he'd like his own shop so he could be his own boss and not work for someone else. With their small savings and some help from my grandparents, they secured the lease on 21 Golborne Road, which had been run as a grocers by Vic Harrison.

Jeannie Rowe (née Searson):

My father was an orphan and left school at 14. I don't know what he did until he joined up for the war. He was a commando and took part in the raid on Saint-Nazaire. He was captured and ended up in a prisoner of war camp. He escaped three times and finally managed to get to Switzerland, from where he was repatriated. My mother worked for a milliner but once the war started, she worked as a telephonist. She was skilled at sewing and made our clothes and also her own.

He met my mother before he went on the raid. She lived in Scotland and also left school at 14. She was one of a family of six and after the war they went to live in Glasgow. I was born there. I came to live in London on my first birthday, 23 October 1945. We had come to London so that my father could find a job. We lived at 253a Portobello Road. It was flat above a shop.

We rented the property from friends of my father who ran a butcher's shop a few doors along the street.

🐦 Charlie Phillips:

I was born in 1944. How British I was; I remember the Queen came to Jamaica after the Coronation in 1953. We travelled a long way to see the Queen. They gave us a Union Jack and we had to say 'God save the Queen'. I was so fascinated to see the royal yacht. I asked my Cub Master, 'How can a big piece of iron like that float?' He said, 'I can't explain that to you now.' This is how I became fascinated with ships. When I was in Kingston, I used to sit on the docks and watch all the immigrant ships come in and take passengers to England. There was migration to Australia, New Zealand. We weren't destitute, a lot of us were well educated. My father and mother came over to England before us. We never thought we were coming here as immigrants we believed so much in the mother country. Some of us was more British than anything else.

In August 1956, we came on a ship called the *Reina Del Pacifico,* which belonged to the Pacific Steam Navigation Company. I came with a group of people who knew my parents and they looked after me on the ship. I landed in Plymouth. We could have got off in Liverpool but a lot of people got off in Plymouth because they were seasick. Then we came up on the boat train that came into Paddington. The first night I came here, my mum and dad was living in a single room because at the time they couldn't get accommodation. No. 9 Blenheim Crescent, that's where I stayed for about two nights, me and about six other people. There was a double room available but it wasn't ready by the time we came. Don't forget at the time, black people couldn't get access to accommodation. Thank God for Rachman. He might have taken some shit but you had a roof over your head.

There was a man stayed over after the war, Leopold Williams at No. 9 Blenheim Crescent. In those days, we didn't have no social worker or nobody to receive us. When he knew the boat train was coming in he would meet people. Some people had no one to meet them and some people had to move on to different addresses in Reading or another popular place was Bradford and another one was Wolverhampton. Slough was another place. The boat trains in those days never come on time, sometimes a day late or a day earlier or five hours late so this man, who was a friend of my dad, helped people who didn't have nowhere to go. He would say, 'Why don't you come and stay with me? You look like you're in transit,' so they would come round to his house.

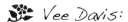 *Vee Davis:*

I had a very good friend back home in Trinidad. In those days they were recruiting young girls for nursing in this country and she was one of those who applied and she got through. I think they took her to Colchester but we'd correspond and I guess she was missing me. I was missing her too and she kept calling me. And so that very year, she came here like April and I came here November 1957. She wanted me to come, so when I come I went straight to 31 Powis Square, and she had come down from Colchester because she was miserable in Colchester, really didn't like it. So she came down to live in London with me.

When I first came over from Trinidad, my God, I was dressed like a circus horse. I'm leaving home to sit on a big ship for two weeks, and I'm wearing white gloves and a white hat. I was coming to the mother country, so I figured I had to look good. I landed at Southampton, took the train to Paddington, and straight into Ladbroke Grove. I remember sitting on the top deck of the bus to see who lived behind this huge wall. It was cloistered nuns. The area got a bit noisy for them so they sold out and the council built some houses.

Margaret Stedman (née Riddick):

My dad was born at No. 79 Kensal Road in 1899 in a row of twelve houses with columns either side of the front door. They could have been beautiful if they'd been done up. His dad was born in Berkshire and moved to London on his own and lived in Ladbroke Grove and worked as an errand boy for a baker's two doors from the Mitre. My dad was too young for the First World War but he signed up anyway and lied about his age. I think he was there eight or nine months before they found out. He got chucked out then he joined up again when he was old enough.

My mum's family are all Notting Hill from way back. My mum's parents lived at No. 10 Stanley Gardens Mews. They had nine children. When my mum and dad got married, they moved back to Kensal Road and that's how I came to be born there. There was twenty years' difference between my mum and my dad.

 Reg Thackeray:

When my mum and dad got married, they lived at 23 St Ervans Road backing on to the railway. That was where they had their daughter, my sister Doreen. My mum came from Southam Street and my dad came from West Row. At No. 23, it was just the basement, two rooms, a kitchen, no bathroom of course, just a tin bath, and an outside lav.

Marg Pithers:

My grandad was born in Latimer Road. He lived most of his life within about 200 yards. He was a road sweeper, a lovely man. My nan had various jobs here there and everywhere. My nan's family were Irish and there were thirteen of them. They lived in Sutton Dwellings at one point. My dad was born there but, for the majority of their married life, they lived in Walmer Road and they only moved when the motorway went through. My grandad and nan were like a pair of munchkins. They were only 5ft, while we were all about 6ft. A lot of my nan's brothers and sisters also lived in Walmer Road.

My dad was one of six children. My dad met my mum when he did his national service in the RAF. My mum was from Dover and all her family was in the Royal or Merchant Navy. My mum and dad got married in the Latimer Road Mission. She refused point blank to have a white wedding, flowers or a photographer. When they got married, they moved in with my nan and grandad until my dad came out of the RAF, then they got a flat in Earl's Court. During the war you had to give up any empty properties because of the housing shortage but the person who owned the house wanted it back after the war, so they moved to Barlby Road opposite the shops at the North Pole end.

Roger Rogowski:

My mum's maiden name was Cook, a family I've traced back to 1780 in Gloucestershire. The Cooks moved to London in the 1860s for what they must have thought would be a better life. My maternal grandad worked almost all of his working life for London Underground as a mechanical engineer.

The Eighth Army might have been the connection that led my mum and dad to move from their first home in Madeley Road in Ealing to Westbourne Park. My dad was a Bren gun carrier driver in one of the Polish infantry divisions in the Eighth Army and, after a spell of peace-keeping duty in Italy at the end of the war, in 1946, he was given a choice of where he wanted to settle. Returning to by now Communist Poland was a dangerous option as stories were already coming back of ex-Allied Polish soldiers being imprisoned, and he thought that the USA was too far, so he decided to settle in England.

He was demobbed in 1947 and, although he was well educated before the outbreak of the war cut his schooling short, his grasp of English must have been basic and he had no English qualifications so he got whatever work was available. He got a job in a bakery after moving to Ealing, where there was a big Polish community. How he and my mum met I don't know but they got married in Ealing Registry Office in November 1951 and my mum continued to work as a cinema usherette until just before I was born.

My dad heard about a flat that was available in Kensal Road in one of two houses owned by an ex-Eighth Army Polish officer, Mr Sohacki, so that's how I came to be born at Paddington General and my birth certificate shows that we were living at 87 Kensal Road. We later moved next door to No. 89. One story from before I was born tells a lot about what the area was like back then. Dad told me he often did the grocery shopping when my mum was expecting me. Back then, there was still rationing and everyone had to register with the grocer of their choice. One day just before they moved, he queued for ages at their grocer in Ealing only to get to the counter and, he suspected because he was Polish with only basic English and a heavy accent, the shop assistant gave him the worst cuts of meat with a lot of fat and tossed the packets on the counter. My dad's English must have stretched to a few choice words because he told him where to stick his meat and walked out. The day they moved to Kensal Road, my dad went to register at the grocer's on the corner of Kensal Road and Elcom Street and he tentatively asked if he could have his ration. The shop assistant, whose attitude was a total contrast to the one in Ealing, said he could have as much as he wanted because a lot of people in the area couldn't even afford to buy their ration.

Mossy Condon:

My grandfather and grandmother lived in Fermoy Road. My grandad had been in the British Army, so he'd been over here for years. My dad had an older brother and three sisters. My dad and his brother got evacuated in the war. My dad went to Ireland – over to my auntie's – and he wouldn't come back after the war. His brother was evacuated to Leicester and, when the two of them got together, one was speaking English and one was speaking Irish. My mum and dad met in Ireland in 1950. My mum was a chambermaid and my dad was an apprentice carpenter, and they got married in 1952 and I was born in 1954. We left Ireland to come over to England in early 1955. My dad came three weeks prior and he got a one-room flat in Hazlewood Crescent. He came from Ireland, where he was earning £3 10s, and when he came over he got a job in Griffith's. He went to £15 a week and that's why they came over. I've got two brothers, Michael and Paul. Paul's nine years younger than me and Michael's eleven years younger.

Barbara Reynolds (née Murray):

My gran, my dad's mum, lived at 63 Bramley Road. Her first husband, Alf Terry, lived in Edenham Street and they moved to Southam Street when they married, where they had their first child, Alice. Alf went to war at a very early age. He was mustard gassed and came home to recuperate. He went back and got killed at Arras when she was carrying her second child, Jessie. She met Tom Murray and they married and she moved in with him at 92 Southam Street on the corner of Adair Road. Tom was a shoe repairer. He had a peg leg, so it was just about the only work he could do. He was also a money lender. He used to charge a shilling in the pound but my gran, being my gran, when they paid the money back to her, she would take it and not charge interest. He used to say, 'We'll never be rich, Alice.' They had two children, Amy and Harry, my dad. I was born at 43 Golborne Gardens in 1954. My dad was a petty officer in the navy in the Second World War.

✍ Bob Crawley:

My dad's family were long-time residents. My great-grandfather lived in Star Street in Paddington in 1845 and my grandparents got married from 84 Wornington Road in 1901. Dad's family were manual workers, having been labourers, chimney sweeps and carmen, like a modern-day delivery driver. My dad had a difficult upbringing. His family were very poor. He was born in 1913 in Talbot Mews and stayed in the area all his life and didn't get married until 1947. He always worked very hard in different jobs. He was always a drinker and wasn't one for going home but he settled down after he got married.

My mum's family originated from Norfolk. Her grandfather moved to Willesden in the late 1800s and her mum and dad settled in Quex Road in Kilburn before moving to the Town. My mum and three of her brothers and sisters were brought up as Catholics but, due to an altercation between my nan and the priest, the next three siblings were brought up as C of E. My mum was 23 when she married my dad.

✍ Christine Smith:

My mother's family, the Freemans, had been in Paddington since the early 1800s and my grandfather, Arthur Thomas, was born in 1881. My parents lived in Shirland Road when they first got married and in 1954 they bought a house in Rainham Road, Kensal Green. My grandfather would come to visit and tell us stories of his time as a soldier in the Royal Artillery in the First World War and of his brother, William, who served in the Royal Berkshire Regiment. My grandad could recall the time the area we lived in was still fields and, because he walked everywhere, he knew every part of it. As a boy he had been a boxer and was well known in amateur circles. I was born in Paddington Hospital on the Harrow Road in 1955, followed by my sister, Cathy, in 1958.

✍ Brian Collins:

My dad came from Ireland. When he came out of the army in 1949, he thought he would try his luck over in England. He came out of Paddington station and walked along Praed Street and he said it felt like coming home. It made a massive impression on him. In 1949 there was a lot of London that needed rebuilding so, because he didn't have a trade when he came out of the army, he thought, 'I can dig ditches, I can do something,' so he became a builder, eventually working for Lovell's.

My mum and dad courted in Ireland and he made the first move coming over to England, then he wrote back and my mum followed later. They settled up in Kilburn very briefly and that's where they were married. Then the chance of two rooms came up in Penzance Place, which were affordable. My dad found the rooms to rent in one of the local newsagent's windows. Mr Baggott was our landlord.

Susan Mcmahon:

My parents came from Ireland in about 1949. My mum was from Galway and my dad was from Clare. My dad got a room in Kilburn with his brother first. My mum and dad met at a dance hall, got married and had six children. There were six of us, I'm the youngest. My brother Paddy was born in 1953, George was born in 1954, my sister Tena in 1955, my brother Noel in 1956, my sister Veronica born in 1959 and I was born in January 1963.

two

Our House

∾ *Frank Hale:*

Our house had four storeys and was owned by the London Co-op. My aunt and uncle and brothers, Jim and Peter, lived in the two rooms on the top floor. They had a gas cooker in my uncle's bedroom. On the next floor down was my grandad and his daughter. There was a gas cooker in his room, and below on the ground floor there were two rooms partitioned off with a toilet on the landing.

There was a woman who lived in the best room in the house at the front of the ground floor. Because we were so hard up, the Co-op asked if we could put her up. She was helping with the rent, paying 6s a week for her room, so we were all squashed in the back room and we had a sitting room and a kitchen in the basement. It must have been a middle upper-class house originally because it had servants' bells in the basement.

After the war, when I was 8 years old, my parents were offered the house for £320 and I remember them having a discussion about what to do. We only paid 13s a week for the whole house and there were repairs to be done so they decided against buying it. A Polish bloke bought it and did it up and offered us money to move out but my parents decided to stay. He sold it to another landlord for £1,100, so he made a tidy profit and we were allowed to stay.

🌱 Ken Farrow:

On the ground floor in Kensal Road, there was a front room and that was my mum's bedroom. There was another bedroom behind that, which was my nan's. Behind that was a scullery, then a kitchen behind that. Outside there was a paved courtyard where the outside toilet was. The printing press building ran along the back between our house and the canal. Upstairs there was a main room and a back bedroom and above that a main room and a back bedroom, so three floors. There was no basement. I had a bath on a Saturday night but I used to go to Wedlake when I started work. I also used to have a shower at the Feather's in Edenham Street, where I did voluntary work.

Kitchen in Kensal House, 1956. Purpose-built blocks such as Kensal House provided a major improvement in living conditions for many moving from Victorian-era multi-occupancy houses.

Jean Russell and baby Jo outside their house in Acklam Road, 1962. The houses in the background were demolished for the building of the Westway.

🌸 Jean Russell (née Hemming):

Until I grew up I didn't realise my mum lived her whole family life in a flat. We called it our house but it was just a front room, a bedroom and a scullery. My mum had a hole in the front door where the letterbox had broken off and everyone would just put their arm in, open the door and walk in. We came from a big family. My mum had eight children but one died. My brother, me and one of my sisters slept in a big bed together, top and tail, with my dad's overcoat as a quilt. We never had enough blankets but we often had a fire lit in the bedroom. My mum and dad stopped sleeping together when my sister was born. We slept like that until we were teenagers. There was a bucket on the floor to wee in.

My aunties and one of my sisters who got married lived upstairs. I vaguely remember an old granny on the middle floor. She must have been my grandad's mum. I was a bit scared of her. I only saw her once that I recall. Auntie Hazel upstairs was a little short woman with blonde hair done in sausage curls at the front, like Betty Grable. She wore size 2 or 3 shoes, often brown and white brogue high heels. She tripped along our street, with her little legs and feet but huge boobs. She called them Betty and Alice. She did her lipstick in a cupid's bow on her top lip, which was very thin. She had a cupboard full of hats. I think she wanted to look smart with her bleached hair, brogues and hat. Her husband Glyn was a Welshman. He sang opera. My mum used to say, 'Listen, Glyn's singing up there.' She named her daughters Vera and Shirley. In the Fifties, Vera got a black boyfriend. My mum and gran always made him welcome but her dad Glyn went mad and, in the end, she gave him up.

✲ Jane Traies:

We lived at 37 Chesterton Road on the corner with Ladbroke Grove. Built onto what must have been the back of the house in Victorian times was the shop so, although we could get to the shop from indoors, the address of the shop was 204 Ladbroke Grove.

Those houses in Chesterton Road were big Victorian houses from the 1870s. They had five floors if we counted the attic and in our time they were divided into flats. We lived on the first floor behind the shop, then above us were two other flats. The flats weren't self-contained. There was just a big staircase going up. We lived in the rooms on the first floor and people would walk past our sitting room and our bedroom.

The whole house belonged to a man called Haskins and we rented the shop and the flat from him, and the families above us did the same. Immediately after the war, in the top flat of our house in Chesterton Road, were a couple of Polish refugees, Mr and Mrs Grodzicki, then on the middle floor was my mother's sister with a baby and her husband newly demobbed. My aunt was suffering from what we would now call post-traumatic stress disorder because she was an army nurse and she had been at the liberation of Belsen. On the first floor was my dad, who had been wounded in the war, and my mum, who was trying to put him back together again.

In the late Forties, we just had two rooms and the back kitchen on the first floor but, from the Fifties, the basement was opened up so we had our living room downstairs in what had been the basement behind the shop and the two rooms on the first floor became bedrooms, so we were better off then. Our dad partitioned the big front room upstairs with a stud wall to make two bedrooms. Jane and I slept in one, John slept in one and our parents slept in the back room. We moved up to Golborne Road for a few years in 1964 and, before we did, we had an outside loo in Chesterton Road. In the winter, Dad would put a paraffin stove out there.

John Traies:

There were two homes. One was 100 Golborne Road, Taverner's newsagents and tobacconists and the other one was 204 Ladbroke Grove, Taverner's newsagents and tobacconists. The shop in Golborne Road was run by Jack and Reenie Taverner, our grandad and nan, and the one in Ladbroke Grove was run by our parents, Blake and Marjorie Traies. No. 100 Golborne Road was multi-occupancy because Reenie's mum lived on the top floor with one brother and the other brother lived downstairs with Jack and Reenie. Our great-granny died in 1953. They also owned 102 Golborne Road, which was a toy shop.

Margaret Burdsey (née Traies):

We had a tiny backyard and I can remember my mum and dad made it as homely as they could. Dad planted pots one year for Kensington in Bloom. It wasn't wonderful. There was damp on the bathroom wall. After a period of time of not being well, our granny and grandad moved away from Golborne Road and they moved down to Brighton, where my granny always wanted to be, so our mum and dad took over the shop in Golborne Road and a cousin came down to take over the shop in Ladbroke Grove. We had the shop refitted when we were up there because it didn't even have a cash register when my granny and grandad were there. They just used to put the money in a wooden drawer. We were in Golborne Road from 1964 to 1967 and in 1967 we went back to 204 Ladbroke. We had an inside loo put in the bathroom and the place had been decorated and our flat partitioned by a wall in the hall, so we were at last self-contained. The shop in Golborne Road was passed to a cousin so it was kept in the family.

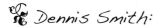 ### Dennis Smith:

We had one bedroom, a sitting room, kitchen and an outside toilet in Victoria Dwellings. There were seven of us. Our tin bath hung over the balcony outside.

Maureen Rafferty (née Coker):

I started in Hazlewood Crescent. We only had one room for sitting and sleeping. It had a big fireplace. We also had a kitchen, which we ate in. Me, my sister Babs, mum and dad all lived there. Later, Gerald and Ray were born in 1954 and 1955 and we moved to Kensal House. In Kensal House we had a living room, three bedrooms, kitchen and a bathroom and toilet. They were quite nice. Mum had a cigarette machine on the wall. Somebody would come along and fill the machine up and take the money out. In them days, there might be twenty quid in there and you would get some money back.

Derek Ford:

Our living accommodation was in Chesterton Road. There were four of us at the top of the house in one room and a tiny kitchen. We shared the toilet with four other families. We had to listen over the bannisters to see if the toilet was free. Sometimes you'd rush down the stairs and meet someone coming up and there would be a fight to get to the toilet.

We had electric but that was only done two or three years before I can remember, maybe around 1952. We also had gas mantles. We were on the top floor. Below us was a very old couple, Mr and Mrs Wilsher. They were Welsh. They had the same as us, a kitchen-cum-scullery where she done her washing and a front room, and they also had a bedroom, so they had three rooms where we only had two. On the next floor down was an Irish chap who lived with his son, Rex, in one room. He was 6 or 7 when I was 10. He had the bedroom-cum-sitting room and diner, just one room, and somebody else had the front room and there was a little kitchen at the back that they both shared. Down in the basement there was a very old lady, Mrs Bullock. Before she passed away, I remember I used to visit her and sit in the armchair by the fire, when I was probably 6 and 7. Just before we moved, an Irish family moved into the basement flat after she died. Their front room was a bedroom, then a little living room, a very big scullery and the garden and an outside lavatory, so they didn't share our toilet.

Richard Rowlands:

I lived at 25 Adair Road from 1946 to 1962, then we moved to Acklam Road, and then I got married and got a flat at 139 Tavistock. We had the middle flat in Adair Road, three rooms and that was it. The bottom three rooms in the basement was condemned. We had a sitting room and a bedroom and I ended up sleeping in the kitchen, which was above the stairs. It was a nightmare. There was the mews out the back of us and I used to hear the cats singing and it sounded like, 'We're coming to get you.' I would never stay in there on my own. I would kick the back door and run down the stairs because it was terrifying.

My dad could have moved. He could have bought that house but all he wanted to do was save his money up for his holidays. He was Welsh and we would go to Wales for our holidays and he would spend all his money there. They moved my mum out of Acklam and pulled it down when they built the Westway and they put her over into the old people's home.

Gwen Nelson (née Martin):

Our lease covered the shop and ground floor, the basement and back yard and the first floor rooms. Above us lived Vic Harrison's daughter, Violet Peck, and her daughter, Beryl, who was a couple of years older than me.

After the lovely house in Lambeth, No. 21 was a huge shock. It was run-down, damp and rickety with brownish wallpaper hanging in large loops all the way up the stairs. Vic Harrison's idea of repairs was to hammer 6-inch nails into everything, including wallpaper that had come loose. The basement of the building consisted of two rooms to the rear with a narrow passage that opened out into a concrete yard. The inner of these rooms had no window and was dripping with green slime. Towards the street was the coal cellar. Coal was delivered by horse and cart, with the street level manhole levered off and coal poured straight down into the cellar. All the rooms at this level had a fine layer of coal dust.

At ground level there was the shop to the front and behind this a storeroom with a coal-fired oven where Mum would heat Cornish pasties and meat pies to sell. It was also very good for putting your feet in on a cold winter's day. A passage ran alongside this with stairs down to the basement and up to the higher levels. It continued on to another room, which was used as our kitchen, and also a communal toilet for all the inhabitants. It was one of Beryl's ploys to sit in there for hours on end reading a comic, refusing to come out until Mum had words with her mum and, after much effing and blinding from Mrs Peck, made her get Beryl out. Beryl would also lay in wait for me on the landing and thump me and try to steal my toys or books, until one day I filled a pint glass mug with water, hid it under my cardigan and then socked her with it, nearly knocking her out. Mrs Peck complained to Mum. After that, Beryl would glare at me but never touched me again.

Halfway up to the first floor the stairs took a right-angled bend. There was a very tall set of French doors that opened out onto the roof of the storeroom. This was one of my favourite spots for playing as I could look out over the Feathers boys' club on Edenham Street. Also Golborne Road, Edenham Street and Southam Street formed a triangle and it was possible to see everyone's backyard. There were no fences around the perimeter and Mum always worried I'd get too near the edge and fall over.

Up on the first floor was a huge lounge that ran the length of the building looking out onto the street. It had two windows with a 12-foot drop and a large fireplace that barely warmed the room. It was so large we had in it our three-piece suite, a large mahogany dining table that could be extended to the size of a table tennis table and a large sideboard with still lots of room to move. To the rear was mum and dad's bedroom with a strip partitioned off by a blanket for me. For a while, Mum tried to use the basement rooms but the damp and dark defeated her and I used them to play my games and keep my growing collection of pets, including a wild rabbit that had a broken back and a tortoise we thought had hibernated until a foul greenish liquid started to emanate from its shell. Among my other pets was a tabby and white cat named Bobby, who was my best friend. He and I would share a bed and he'd cuddle up to me with both arms round my neck.

Jeannie Rowe (née Searson):

The flat in Portobello Road was two floors and quite spacious. It was on top of a shoe shop. On the first floor was a kitchen and dining room. There was a small fire in the corner with a metal attachment on it. The kettle sat there so there was always some hot water. There was a trestle table and the floor was covered with lino. Next door was a living room with a fireplace. We had a much smarter dining table in there with matching chairs. It must have been a biggish room because I remember I got a bike for Christmas when I was 7 and being able to ride it round the room. Upstairs on the landing was a tiny toilet with a wash handbasin. It only had cold water. We didn't have any hot water in the flat. There were two bedrooms; one for my parents and one for us three children.

Charlie Phillips:

After two nights in England, we got a double room at 15 Bassett Road. It was a front room that was partitioned with a curtain. I had a folding bed. My mum and dad had a double bed. There was a communal kitchen on the landing and we had to share the bath. You had to put the penny in the meter for the geyser. For heating, you had a paraffin heater and a kettle on the top, so when you got up in the morning you had a bit of warm water so you could have a wash. It was a cultural shock. Some of them wanted to go home but we thought we would stick it out for five years.

Coming out of your house straight onto the street. We never had that in the West Indies. It got warm four days after we arrived. In the Caribbean, automatically you'd take your shoes off and play. I got told off. 'You're in England now. Put your shoes on.' Then we moved to No. 50 Bonchurch Road, then we had a bigger flat now in the basement. It had a big bay window and we had to share the house with three other families. There was a communal kitchen on the landing.

Vee Davis:

I remember looking around for somewhere to live and you see all these signs with 'No blacks, no children, no Irish, no dogs', and you knew then that you ain't going to ask. They say that there's rooms to let but you're not going to ask because you know that you're black, so keep out.

Michael was a guy I'd known from Trinidad. Michael de Freitas. They used to call him Michael X. So when we met it was like in those days you see a black face you say, 'Oh my god, you're here, when you come? Where you living, girl?' So I was pleased to see Michael, but then he said, when I asked about looking for somewhere to live, he sent me to go to this man. He didn't call a name. He just give me the address. He told me to go down to this man's office, in his basement off Bayswater, with a tiger skin on the floor. It was Peter Rachman. I said: 'Mister, we're looking for somewhere to live.' He said, 'For business?'

I was so green and stupid. All I said to the man, 'Mister, I ain't got no money to open no business.' And you could see he must think I was daft or something, I can't be bothered with her. He said sorry and that was it, but a few weeks after, I met Michael and he gave me hell. He was like, 'What's the matter with you? They took the girl out the country but they can't take the country out of you. You're sitting on a pot of gold and you don't know.' There were only a few black girls in the area. He was nasty to me and then it clicked. It all come together that this business the man had asked about was to go on the streets.

I moved into the Rachman house anyway. I used to see henchmen come to the house for the rent, one was Mr Hughes. It was never Rachman because anything go wrong in the house and you want to tell them, the bulb gone or the tile buckled or anything, he's supposed to come and fix it. It was a furnished apartment. It was a hell of a time. You don't dare complain. Who you going to complain to and you're so glad you've got a roof over your head. Just make sure you work and you get the money to pay him. I remember only that time I saw him when Michael sent me to him but otherwise I wouldn't have known who is Rachman.

Margaret Stedman (née Riddick):

We lived at 88 Kensal Road. The outside toilet was out on a flat roof two flights down and there was a flight of stairs to a cold water tap, and that's how we lived. We had two rooms, a bedroom and a room that we ate in, and our kitchen was out on the landing. I slept with my mum and dad. We had a tin bath in front of the fire. Our house backed onto the Grand

Union Canal. Looking back, it was very basic and not good at all. That's why we moved. My uncle lived in Lancaster Road opposite what became Basing Street Studios and, when he moved out to Surrey, we took over his flat because there was more space. That had a kitchen-cum-lounge and two bedrooms. I had my own bedroom, which was luxury. We were only there six months when my dad died. He was 59 and I was only 12.

Later, I got married and had my son and we all lived in Lancaster Road. Then they put a bathroom in when my son was 4 or 5, another luxury. My rent was £2 11s in 1964 and it went up to £4 when they put the bathroom in. My friend in Lansdown Crescent paid £20 a month. In those days, out of your wages, you could pay the rent and the basics and still afford to go out to the pub. There was a very old wall at the end of the backyard and, one day, the wall just fell down along five houses' backyards. It sounded like a bomb going off.

❀ Ray Matthews:

I was born in 1947. We lived at No. 89 Sirdar Road. There were five of us in two bedrooms and a kitchen-cum-living room, gas lights in all the rooms and the only real heating was a fire in the kitchen. At the back in the scullery was a copper where mum had to boil the water for washing. In the kitchen was a sink with just a cold tap, so every morning it was a wash in cold water with Lifebuoy soap. The bedrooms were freezing cold in the winter, ice forming on the windows. Our toilet was by the scullery and rats would come up the toilet after heavy rain. It was very scary as a kid.

❀ Babs Coker:

I don't remember much from Hazlewood Crescent because our family moved from there to Kensal House in Ladbroke Grove when I was very young. From Kensal House we moved to Acklam Road as we had a three-bedroom flat and there was five of us. We used to heat our home with coke, which you collected from the gasworks near Kensal Road. We also used a paraffin heater and bought paraffin from the oil man who came round selling.

🎋 Alan Peverall:

The first house I lived in was 28 Golborne Gardens. My only memory of that time was a lovely lady called Ada, who only had one arm. I remember she looked after me when my mum died in 1955.

We then moved to 167 Southam Street next to the school. There were three families living in the house including us and Mr and Mrs Choules and Stephen, their grandson. I can't remember the name of the family on the middle floor. We lived on the ground floor. My dad and stepmum slept in the first room. We were never allowed to play in there. The middle room was a kitchen and living room, then there was a small room at the back where me and my brother slept. We had an outside toilet in the backyard. We had to creep down the stairs to the basement to go to the toilet, which was very scary at night. The basement had empty rooms. They were in a poor state with no paint on the walls, just brickwork, and it was very damp and smelly. There was also a coal cupboard in the basement under the street.

🌿 Reg Thackeray:

We were still living at 23 St Ervans Road when the basement and ground floor at No. 21 became available, so we moved there. In 1960, my parents bought the whole house freehold for £900 so then we had ten rooms. My dad had the basement for his workshop. He loved it. He could hide down there and dismantle and repair things that he picked up as part of his house clearance business. He did it as a hobby not for money.

🌿 Roger Rogowski:

When I was very young, I seemed to have the run of the house with the blessing of all the other tenants. Below, in the basement flat, were the Cullen family, dad Con, mum Mary and son Cornelius, which was also shortened to Con. They had a separate entrance to their flat down a few steps from the road and an internal entrance on our floor under the first flight of stairs.

Their basement flat was almost identical to ours with a large living room at the front, a large bedroom at the rear, a corridor running front to back with the living and bedroom doors on the left and a lavatory on the right and, in a rear extension narrower than the house, a kitchen and a bathroom, which was accessible through a door at the back of the kitchen. They had sole access to the coal cellar. I remember the rumble of coal being tipped into the cellar by the coal man, who delivered sacks from the back of his horse-drawn cart through the manhole at the bottom of the external flight of steps. The Cullens also had a back yard – we never called it a garden – at the rear of the house, which was just a scrubby rectangle of grass where they hung their washing and Con and I let off our fireworks on bonfire night.

As we had a shared front door and all of the other tenants walked in and out past our living room door, which had a lock on it and the room was locked at night but left open during the day. There was a code for knocking on the front door. One knock was for us, two knocks for the floor above us and three knocks for the top floor. The living room was originally full of heavy, brown Victorian furniture and had an open fireplace, which I remember was a major performance to light, involving a sheet of newspaper being held in front of the fireplace to draw the flames, with the newspaper usually catching light. Our fireplace was eventually boarded up and replaced by an electric fire with a not very convincing coal-effect light. When I was very young, I remember drawing in the condensation on the windows in the winter and found that, afterwards, my fingers smelt of soot, which must say something about the quality of the air we were breathing. We had gas mantles either side of the fireplace, although they were never used because my parents thought they were dangerous.

Barry Bucknell, maybe the first TV DIY personality, had a major influence on my parents and, piece by piece over time and with the blessing of our landlord, my dad chopped up the old furniture and replaced it gradually with modern-style furniture, a coffee table with spindly legs, pine dining table, chairs and sideboard, three-piece suite and two rattan easy chairs. A lot of this new furniture was bought from Wheatlands in Harrow Road. In the days before credit cards, it was common to make major purchases with a deposit followed by monthly cash payments made to the tallyman, who knocked on the door to collect payments either weekly or monthly. Called hire purchase, my mum and dad bought all of their new furniture this way, setting out the exact money on the mantelshelf for the tallyman before his visit.

Family meals were always eaten in the kitchen as the dining table in the front room was for entertaining guests. Our Sunday lunch was always on the table at the same time every week and a portable transistor radio later provided the soundtrack to Sunday lunch with the *Clitheroe Kid* or *Round the Horne* followed by *Two-* and later *Three-Way Family Favourites*. Barry Bucknell's evil influence struck again when my mum decided to paint the old kitchen table bright pink. Unfortunately, it seemed to be the kind of paint that never really dried and it went the way of the rest of the old brown furniture shortly afterwards to be replaced by a formica-topped table with spindly tapered legs.

Our bathroom was beyond the kitchen and was just about big enough for the bath and a huge menacing-looking geyser suspended from the wall. As another part of our Sunday ritual, I had a bath once a week whether I needed it or not. At other times, after playing outside, usually in one street or another, my exposed parts, face, hands and knees, would be scrubbed by my mum and I remember at least one time when the dirt must have been especially stubborn, she cleaned my knees with Vim.

My dad would get his decorating equipment from Hibberd's, a hardware shop at the Kensal Road end of Golborne Road, where Holmfield House now stands. As we lived in rented accommodation, his DIY activities were usually limited to decorating and destroying old furniture but, one year, he decided the windowsill outside our front room bay window needed improvement and he built a window box. Hibberd's was like the shop in *The Two Ronnies'* four candles sketch and seemed to sell everything. We also bought our paraffin in the winter for our portable paraffin heater from there. Anyway, as the window box was my dad's first major DIY effort, he bought the works: a hammer, saw, tape measure and square as well as wood and nails, which were sold by weight. The soil came from the yard at the back of our house and it couldn't have done the plants any harm as there was always a colourful display every summer, which must have been a minor landmark in our otherwise grim row of Victorian houses.

Upstairs from our flat was an intermediate floor with a bathroom and toilet facing the rear of the house, which was shared by all of the other tenants. One further flight of stairs up to the first floor was a two-roomed flat occupied by a family, living room in front and bedroom to the rear with a kitchenette on the landing and, a further two flights up to the second floor were two bedsits, one in the front and one in the back. One bedsit had a kitchenette on the landing and the other had a kitchenette in an extension that looked like a garden shed on top of the flat room of the communal bathroom, up a narrow flight of temporary-looking stairs. The people on the top floor seemed to move in and out on a frequent basis. There was a single mother and newly born baby who had moved from Helston in Cornwall, who left her husband and older children behind. I'm sure there was a story there. Before her in the same bedsit was a woman in her early twenties, Anna, who had beautiful long blonde hair and who would sometimes sit me down and read me stories. She was saving to travel to the Greek islands, with Mykonos as one of her intended stops. Before she left, as a parting gift, she gave me a book on Greece. My mum much later told me that Anna was a prostitute.

My impression is that visits to our neighbours and developing trust, at least in trusted adults, was encouraged on both sides. My young brother Chris remembers, when he was pre-school age, being told by our mum to climb the stairs and knock on the door of the family living upstairs, which he did reluctantly. He remembers a smiling face when the door opened and being given sweets for both of us, obviously something they'd arranged in advance.

Mossy Condon:

We moved into 23 Hazlewood Crescent in 1955, then we moved to 11. They were both just one big bedroom. We slept, ate and lived in there. We had a round oil heater that we cooked on top of. We had an outside toilet. You had to go down to the yard, so it wasn't very comfortable at night time, so we had a potty under our bed. You'd empty it out in the mornings when you got up because it would be too cold to go outside. The winters in them times were very cold and there was always snow around in the late Fifties and early Sixties. The reason we moved down was because No. 23 was the last house next to the bomb site and they were frightened the house was going to fall down so they moved everybody out of there and they moved us down to No. 11. All the buildings were connected with an outside balcony on every house. You could get on one balcony and walk right the way along.

We never got moved out of there until 1965, when we moved into Hazlewood Tower, which was beautiful because we went from one room where we ate, slept, watched our television and when we moved, I had my own bedroom, my mum and dad had their own bedroom, we had a sitting room, an indoor toilet and a bath, so we could have a bath every day of the week, not once on a Friday after Dad had finished.

🌿 Barbara Reynolds (née Murray):

We had the first floor and the second floor, so we were a bit squashed in. The rent man come one day in 1955. The man laughed at my dad and they had a bit of an argument. My dad pushed him and he had to go to court. The clerk of the court said to my dad, 'The judge is a navy man, play on the navy. Tell him you were a petty officer in the war.' My dad went to Marylebone Court and the judge heard the case and adjourned it until two o'clock so my dad went back at two o'clock and the judge said, 'I've been into your navy record and you're going to get a house in Swindon.' My dad said, 'Where the bloody hell's Swindon?'

When it was time to move, I was very ill in hospital. I was only 18 months old so my grandad told my dad to move the family to Swindon and collect me when I'm better, but I never moved down. We had a massive front room behind my grandad's shop and our bedrooms were upstairs and then upstairs again was the Ingarfields, Janet, Lizzie, Tommy, and Jessie and Tom, their mum and dad.

My grandad died when I was 3. When my grandad was very ill, Jessie used to bring down beautiful meals and feed him while my gran was doing other things. My gran used to stay up with him all night. After my grandad died, my gran took a job at Joe Lyons' cleaning while I was being looked after by my cousin Jean. We left the shop and moved to 139 Southam Street because there was only me and my gran. We had a bathroom, toilet, kitchen and bedroom there. Our house in Southam Street was knocked down just before I started secondary school in 1965, then we moved to Southam House and we had a kitchen, bathroom, toilet, bedroom and lounge.

🐦 Bob Crawley:

For the first five years of my life, I lived at 24 Golborne Gardens. Our house was a three-storey tenement with a basement and was shared with two other families. The basement was empty. Old Mrs Bruce lived on the first floor, Maud and David Bruce on the second floor, and my family had the two rooms at the top. The backyard was used as a home for racing pigeons. One room served as a bedroom for the five members of the family – me, my elder sister, brother, mum and dad – and the other room was a small kitchen. The kitchen had a large iron range that was never used, a small sink with only a cold water tap, a small table and four chairs and a kitchen cupboard. Hot water had to be boiled up on the gas cooker. The gas cooker was located on the landing between the two rooms and we shared a basement toilet with the other families. I wasn't allowed to use the toilet, which was down three floors and supposedly visited by rats, and I had to make do with a potty as did my elder brother and sister after bedtime.

There would be the front door key on a bit of string so anyone could let themselves in. In the basement they had a front room, which they used as a bedroom and then a primitive bathroom and a kitchen. As a consequence of our house in Golborne Gardens being designated for demolition, we moved to Bramley House in Bramley Road, not far when looking back but it did mean I had to leave St Andrew's School and go to Thomas Jones School, a five-minute walk away, something I did from a very early age without any parental supervision. After a couple of years, we moved back to Bosworth House in Bosworth Road, so I returned to St Andrew's School.

Brian Collins:

My mum and dad occupied three rooms in the top part of the house, which was three storeys, at 14 Penzance Place just off Princedale Road. We had a kitchen out on the landing, which was minute, with a gas cooker, an Ascot heater and a sink. We didn't have a bathroom. There were two small bedrooms and a living room. Another family, mother, father and three children occupied the lower floor of the same house. When the people downstairs moved out, they had more room so we moved downstairs and had to pay a little bit more rent. Then my aunt and uncle and their three children, my cousins, moved into the top bit of the house. I would go round my friends' houses and they had less than we did.

Susan Mcmahon:

We lived at 26 Tavistock Road. My cousins lived downstairs on the ground floor and we lived on the first floor. We had a great big living room, a bedroom, kitchen, bathroom and toilet. I slept with my mum and dad and my sisters in one room. My brothers' bedroom was on the same floor as two old ladies, Mrs Farr and Elsie, who lived on the top floor. Mrs Farr was a dear old lady. Her room was packed with stuff with a double bed in the middle of it. She never came out of her room. She always seemed to be in bed.

My mum was very friendly with her and used to take her up sandwiches. Elsie had black hair and used to wear red lipstick and a fur coat with nothing on underneath. She would often get drunk and start on everyone. My mum was a friend to all of them and she went back to visit Elsie after we moved, before she went into a home because she had nowhere else to go.

three

Home Life

ॐ Frank Hale:

My mum was a very good cook and organiser. She would do mostly stews. Her rabbit stew with dumplings and pearl barley was a favourite until the myxomatosis came in. We never went without food, although money was scarce. My two older brothers were eighteen months apart but then there was a ten-year gap to me, so I never got handed down any of their clothes. I always had second-hand clothes because we couldn't afford new clothes but I never went without.

ॐ Ken Farrow:

I had four younger sisters and two older brothers by 1957. My mum remarried in 1956. I was mum's favourite. I hated it, not that I didn't love her but I hated being her favourite. Everyone else used to pick on me. My sisters made my life hell and my stepdad didn't like it either. My younger stepbrother was a bit of a bully until I kicked him in the nuts one day. Every Saturday morning he would give me half a crown and make me run to Holm's to get him half a dozen jam doughnuts, tuppence ha'penny each. He would sit there and eat the lot. Mine was the pleasure of watching him eat them. He was a teddy boy. He fancied himself in his jacket, tight trousers and his quiff. He used to get into trouble with the police. I might go into Holm's and get a roll for breakfast if I had a few pennies for my breakfast on the way to Cardinal Manning School.

On Saturday, I would be sent out to buy 20lb of potatoes to last Sunday and through the week. During the week it would be things like neck of mutton stew, mutton chops or pease pudding and faggots or saveloys from Hamperl's. On Sunday, it would be a roast shoulder of mutton or shoulder of veal, the cheapest cuts, and a heap of baked potatoes and cabbage. We had school dinners when I started at Cardinal Manning. They had their own dining hall and we had a main meal and a pudding there, so I didn't have a big meal in the evening.

When my mum remarried, because my stepfather was a dustman and in those days they used to do the old compliments of the season round all the houses, he would bring home £50 or £60 in tips at Christmas. He had a lucrative round, Warwick Avenue and Maida Vale way. He worked out of a yard up by Royal Oak. He would drink a lot of it but we would have a big turkey for Christmas and mum would spend a fortune on the catalogue and wrap all the presents on Christmas Eve.

Bob Crawley peeping around the corner with Uncle Connie Moroney, Great Aunt Ivy Ifield and Mum José in Shaftesbury House, which stood on the corner of Golborne Gardens and Adair Road, 1960.

From the left, Sheila Thompson, Charlotte Thompson and Doreen Mustoe playing cards at home in Lonsdale Road, 1959, a common scene in pre-television days.

✤ Jane Traies:

When we joined the Brownies you had to pass certain tests and one of the parts of them was that you had to show that you could light a fire using only two matches, and that was something that every little girl in the Brownies aged 7 needed to be able to do so our mums had to teach us how to do that and write to say we had done it. That was our only form of heating other than a paraffin heater. The Esso Blue man used to come round selling paraffin and then there was the coal man. My mum used to light the fire every morning in the winter. We had an Ascot for hot water and a coal cellar. We used to say, 'Can we run down and watch the coal go in the cellar?' and our mum would say, 'No you'll get dirty.'

Our gran had curling tongs that looked like a pair of scissors that you had to heat up in a flame. You had to try them out on a bit of brown paper and, if it singed the paper, they were too hot. Although we think we had a hard life, we were well off compared to most of the children we went to school with. We not only had a car but we also had a television with a 9-inch screen by the time of the Coronation in 1953 and people came in to watch it.

✿ Jean Russell (née Hemming):

If I wanted a private wash, I had to take a bowl of water in the bedroom. I went to Wedlake every now and again. I was having my once a week bath in the tin bath in the kitchen. One day, my mum said, 'Come on Jean, get in the bath,' and all my dad's friends were sitting round the table playing crib and drinking beer. My sister had moved in upstairs by then because she was married. I was about 13 and my sister said, 'Are you still making her have a bath in front of people?' My mum said, 'They've seen it all before, they've all got kids.' She had no empathy at all but I suppose she had a hard life. My mum was a hard woman. She was horrible to us and got worse when we were older. She didn't seem to be able to cope with teenagers. She would put my dinner over my head in temper sometimes but everyone loved her. She was a bit of a girl and a laugh to everyone else.

We used the bagwash in Herries Street. It was also a dry-cleaners and almost everyone I knew worked there at some time. I used to be sent to bring the bagwash home. It was only the next street. I'm sure it wasn't soaking wet or I couldn't have carried it. I think it was spin-dried. My mum sent all the whites in one bag and it came back lovely and white. I can't remember if she sent coloured items. Other times she'd wash it all herself in our old copper, then rinse in the big old scullery sink, then mangle it all and hang it on the line or across the kitchen above our heads while we ate dinner.

I only had one boyfriend before I married and that was my husband, who was a Kilburn boy. I was only 17 when I first met him. We had to get married like you did in those days. My mum didn't want me to marry him. I had two baby boys. He told me one day that he didn't want to be married. He said, 'I shouldn't have married you.' He used to insult me and call me ugly. One day, he said, 'I'm not going to work anymore. I've had enough of this. I'm too young to be married and settle down.' I had to get a job because he wouldn't go to work and I had no money. My sister used to give me ten bob to get the kids some dinner, so I went and got this job off Kilburn Lane in the evenings and that's where I met this bloke.

He was West Indian. He kept going after me and telling me I was lovely and, of course, it was music to my ears and so he started putting notes on my work desk saying 'I love you' and 'You're beautiful'. I was still only young and had no experience of men so I started meeting him in secret. All the women at work liked him so I felt privileged that he was after me. This bloke invited me to his friend's house after work and they got me drunk. I wasn't used to drink because we were so strictly brought up. They gave me a long glass of something. I don't know what it was. I was legless. I couldn't walk. I fell on the floor. I couldn't go home. I collapsed on the bed and stayed the night. In the morning I said, 'I can't go home. What am I going to do?' I wanted my children. I was distraught.

He got a room in Wornington Road and we moved in together. I was heartbroken really. None of them would have anything to do with me but my sister took my two little boys. I lived like that for a long time, heartbroken, and then I got pregnant in 1962 and he started beating me up and he stabbed me in the arm. I got cracked ribs. He was a violent schizophrenic. He used to go berserk. I had nobody to support me because I'd gone off with a black man and it wasn't done then, so all my family disowned me. My brother called me a whore. I had nobody but just other white women that went with black men and they were all the friends I had.

He was very self-possessed. I had nothing to wear. He stole my maternity money to buy clothes with so he looked smart. My mum came to see me one day and she said, 'What happened to you?' After I'd had the baby, it was off the Golborne Road, he took my little girl and I chased him. I grabbed the baby off him and he pushed me under a car and kicked me in the face and busted my nose open. There was a crowd standing around and nobody did anything. Someone called an ambulance and they took me away and I had eight stitches. He got one month in jail for that and came out and beat me up again. He said, 'I can introduce you to some prostitutes. It's only business, then you can get some money to get a nice house and then you can get your boys.' I was shocked. He dragged me round the streets one day and introduced me to some prostitutes and then I ran away. He dragged me back. I went to the police and they said, 'Have you done it?' When I said no, they said, 'When you do, come back because we can't do anything until you do.'

I got a room in Silchester Terrace but someone told him where I lived. It was that winter when it was freezing with lots of snow. He came up the stairs. I was so shocked I lost my ability to speak I was so terrified. He got me and the baby and dragged me through the streets to Carlton Vale. A police car came past and I wanted them to stop but I dare not speak. We got to the house. There was one of his friends downstairs and I said to him, 'Take the baby because he's going to beat me up.' He dragged me up the stairs and the beating I got, I must be really strong because it's a wonder I'm not dead because he kicked me, he hit me with a bottle against the head and I had black eyes. His friend came up and looked at me with great pity. In the morning, out of the blue, he said, 'Take this ten bob and get me some steak for breakfast.' I couldn't believe he was letting me go. He said, 'Leave the baby,' because he didn't think I would leave him without taking the baby. I ran and ran to where my cousin worked in the cleaners and I said, 'Hide me in the back.' She said, 'Go home to your mum, she's not going to see you out.'

I ran all round the back turnings to my mum in Beethoven Street. She took me to the doctor and he said, 'Say the word and I'll go to court to give evidence.' I said, 'No, I'm too frightened.' He came to my mum's house kicking the door, so I moved to Brighton but he broke into my sister's house and found the address and came to Brighton. I finally went to the police after he beat me again. I was beaten and cut so badly I looked like a piece of liver. I kidnapped my sons from school and took them home to my mum. I went to the welfare and they gave me a place called Morning Lane in Hackney.

🌿 *Pauline Clark (née Harding):*

Some people never had baths in their homes. We only had a tin bath, which we all shared. Me being the youngest had a deep bath but you can imagine what it was like after we all had a bath. School uniform was to last a week. When I got home from school, I had to hang it up. The only heat in the house was a coal fire in the front room. We only had a cold cupboard to keep the meat and milk. Saturday's dinner was pie and mash, sausage and mash on occasions and pease pudding.

Derek Ford:

My older brother, who was born in 1941 and six years older than me, and I would fight to put our feet in the gas oven to keep warm. We had an old stone sink that only had cold water. There was no hot water. We had the bath hanging outside on the wall on a nail. We all bathed on a Sunday and the youngest bathed last in the same water that the eldest bathed in. My mum, dad, my brother, then me. Because my dad didn't have a lot of money, both my brother and I used to have cardboard in the bottom of our shoes to make them last a bit longer. God forbid it was wet, then all the cardboard would get soaked, but we were looked after and well fed, probably not by today's standards.

Alan Warner:

Our home was the bottom floor of a three-floored house. We had two rooms and a scullery. We used to sleep three or four to a bed and in winter we had coats as blankets. Mealtimes were fun. If you were unlucky, you got your dinner on a saucepan lid. On Sundays, dinner was delayed until the Falcon pub in Kilburn Lane closed at two o'clock and Dad had gone to Poppa Lord's seafood stall outside the pub. On many Sunday teatimes, we had winkle sandwiches after Dad had pulled off the little covers on them and stuck them on our faces. There were four of my dad's sisters living with their families in Beethoven Street, Iris, Edna, Ethel and Lena, many cousins and my lovely Nanny Warner. I used to pop in sometimes after school to visit and odd times do any washing up that was there.

Richard Rowlands:

My brothers were Raymond and Derek. Raymond was six years older. Derek was four years older and Raymond was a really good footballer. Pie and mash was one and ninepence, fish and chips was two bob and that was a treat for us. My mum used to give me four KitKats in the morning and I had three sugars in my tea, so no wonder I got diabetes. We had a tin bath and I was the sixth one in it. There was five of us but they used to put the dog in before me. Our toilet was down in the garden. It was pitch black at night and my old man would come down and scratch on the door and frighten me to death. He was afeared of nothing.

 *Gwen Nelson (née Martin):*

We were fortunate in only having one other family with which to share the above-shop accommodation. On Saturday night, the galvanised bathtub would be lifted off the wall in the hallway and lugged into the kitchen where it would be filled from saucepans and kettles boiled on the gas stove. I had the first, quick bath, then mum with the addition of more hot water and finally dad after some water had been ladled out and still more hot added. The rest of the week, in the words of my grandmother, I 'washed down as far as possible, up as far as possible and then washed my possible.'

Clothing was washed in a galvanised tub with a wooden scrubbing board and a bar of hard, yellow Sunlight soap. No such thing then as a daily change of clothes, although knickers were probably changed a couple of times a week and the crotch rinsed out and hung up to dry overnight. At most, clothing was washed weekly or taken to the bagwash on the corner of Golborne and Southam Street. The bagwash took in your clothing and returned it to you later that day to be dried at home. Mum would load the bag on my pushchair and wheel it along the road, then retrace her steps that afternoon. Frequently someone else's odd sock or handkerchief would turn up among your wash, or some item of yours would be missing. From inside the shop, one could look out the back and see the vats of hot, soapy water where the laundry would be stewed into submission. Anything delicate was washed at home and hung on a clothes line that extended out the back window on a pulley system and was affixed at its far end to a pole rising up from the backyard. This worked well until the rope broke and everything tumbled down into the filthy yard and had to be retrieved and rewashed. People kept themselves clean to the best of their abilities considering the appalling conditions in which they lived.

Jeannie Rowe (née Searson):

My sister and brother were both born in the house. I was sent to stay with relatives on these occasions. We obviously didn't have much money but I think we ate well. Living on the market, there was a plentiful supply of fruit and vegetables. I remember chicken being a very special treat because it was expensive. We didn't have it often. There was a baker's shop across the road but my mother cooked with pastry and made plenty of puddings. We ate bread but you could only have butter or jam on your bread, but not both. I remember dried eggs and the special orange juice provided for new babies. Sugar was on ration until I was 8. I remember the excitement that caused when the ration came off. We could go down to Maynard's, the sweet shop in Ladbroke Grove, and buy sweets.

Life with three children was very labour intensive. My mother washed on Mondays, probably having changed the beds. She had to heat all the water so the tin bath and any large pans were put on the stove to heat the water. The clothes were washed and then put through the mangle. Then they were hung outside on the roof, where there was a washing line. It was a flat roof that was over the shop. We played out there when the weather was good. If it was raining we had an old-fashioned pulley in the kitchen. Then on Tuesdays everything had to be ironed. Cleaning must have taken quite a lot of time because we had no appliances.

The coal man used to deliver coal in his horse-drawn cart to the coal hole in the pavement. My father would have to carry the coal up the spiral staircase to the first floor. We also had heating from paraffin stoves. I remember a hardware shop on the opposite corner where we bought the paraffin. It was run by Mr and Mrs Holdsworth.

On Sunday evenings my mother used to heat up water for the tin bath. We all took turns and my father used to wrap me in a towel and hold my head under the tap to rinse the shampoo off. We towel-dried our hair and then sat near the fire before going to bed. Night clothes were warmed on the fire guard because there was no heating in the bedrooms. At home I learned to read before I started school and I could also knit. I played with dolls and made clothes for them. I also read a lot. We didn't have any books at home but the library was at the end of the road, so I was a regular visitor.

𝒮 Charlie Phillips:

People would tie the front door key on a piece of string, so you could just let yourself in. I was a single kid but I had plenty of auntie and uncle figures, which you don't see any more. This is a tradition that's dying out. Our parents didn't talk to us or tell us anything. If I asked them anything they would tell me to shut up. Little kids should be seen and not heard. They never talked about their past. That was true of a lot of working-class parents. People would say, 'They come over here and live five to a room,' but we never had anywhere to live. In those days the council didn't give you flats, so we had to fend for ourselves.

൙ Margaret Stedman (née Riddick):

There was always someone who could play the piano. My uncle could play and, when he did, you would sit there with your mouth open listening. He could even play 'Rhapsody in Blue'. The people downstairs had a piano and my parents would go there after coming back from the pub. There was something that everyone could do so everyone did a turn. Uncle George could belt out a song. He would pull out one or two and no matter how much praise he got, he wouldn't do any more. There was a song that started, 'Why waste those tears over me little girl, those eyes were not meant to cry,' and I've never found it yet. I can remember him singing that song over and over but I can only remember those two lines.

My dad was married before he met my mum and they had a little girl who died and then my mum and dad had another daughter before me who also died young, so when I came along he wrapped me up in cotton wool. I used to get farmed out to Camberley until I was about 13 for the school holidays. My dad was a softy and would pick up waifs and strays. One Christmas Day, he's gone over to the pub and had a few and brought home this boy who said he'd got nowhere to go. His name was Johnny Clugston and he lived in Adair Road. My dad said, 'I've been round the house and I know he hasn't got any dinner.' He described the scene and said, 'I've got to bring him back and he'll have dinner with us.' It was Christmas Day and my mum was peeved but Johnny became my friend because I had no brothers and sisters. He was a year older than me and he became my protector.

One Christmas, I was bought a doll from The Singing Doll Company. It played a small record in the tummy. They made them in a factory in Harrow Road near St Mary's Hospital. I was a teenager when I saw Johnny Clugston for the last time. He said he remembered, if my dad saw children playing out in the street, he would say, 'You're all going to the newsreel,' and he would take them along to see the cartoons at the cinema in Praed Street. We called it the newsreel because they showed Pathé News between the cartoons. Five or six kids and me would all be trooping up to the station and get out at Edgware Road. Sometimes it would start out just me and my cousin and by the time we got to the station there would be half a dozen of us.

✼ Ray Matthews:

Life was hard. My dad would fetch home dog ends and I would take the paper off of them and put the baccy in a tin with a bit of potato peel to keep it moist. He smoked Boar's Head tobacco, or as he called it, Pig's Bonce. My dad's family were always up to some scam and we would often have stuff come in our back door, which opened onto the alley behind the house. All sorts of stuff from sewing machines to rolls of suit material would appear and disappear overnight. I don't know what else my family were involved in, only that it was totally illegal. The only time my darling mum went absolutely mad at my dad was one evening, she was looking for something in a drawer and she froze. When my dad came in, she screamed at him, 'What the bleedin' 'ell you playing at? Get that out of 'ere now.' It was a gun wrapped in a tea towel. It went straight out for someone to look after.

✿ Babs Coker:

Christmas was always a real treat. My family all lived in the area, so my parents took it in turns to spend Christmas in each other's houses. My nan and aunt lived in Swinbrook Road, my other nan lived in Wornington Road and my other aunt lived in Bevington Road. One of my nans was then moved to Hazlewood Tower and every week she would go out and buy her Guinness for the week but this particular week, she came home with her Guinness for the week, got in the lift and the lift broke, so she was stuck. They called out the fire brigade but they took so long, when they finally opened the doors, my nan was drunk because she had drunk all her Guinness for the week.

❦ Reg Thackeray:

There was no such thing as leisure time in those days. We might go to the seaside for the day, Brighton or Margate maybe, but that was all. We had a car, a Vauxhall estate registration No. 474GLC. We always had a telly. The first colour telly we had was bought in 1966 from Wheatland's in the Harrow Road. It was about £500 and was always going wrong. It was a waste of money. My dad bought it from Mr Archer, the manager. If my dad wanted something from there, Mr Archer would send it. Money wasn't asked for and my dad would pay later because my dad had a very good name anywhere. Sometimes he paid in instalments but he bought the telly outright.

❦ Marg Pithers:

I was the eldest and my nan looked after me when I was a baby when my mum went to work. One time, I was in my pram all dressed in white and my nan put a bag of coal in with me and, when my mum got home, I was all covered in coal dust. When the others came along, my mum became a dinner lady because the hours fitted in with school. We had a season ticket at St Mark's and Princess Louise Hospitals because we were always having accidents and cutting ourselves. My sister still has a massive dent on her head where a swing went into her.

Our front door faced our neighbour's front door and there were two flats downstairs, so there was a courtyard where we played making a hell of a noise. Someone left the gate open and my sister wandered out, got to the bus stop and got on the bus. She was only 2. By this time, we'd realised she was missing. Us and the neighbours were tearing the place over looking for her and this was in the days before we had a phone. The police turned up and said she's sitting in Acton police station. Acton was the last stop on the No. 7. They realised they'd got this little girl sitting on her own so they took her to the police station and when we went to get her, she was sitting there eating ice cream.

Our neighbours opposite us downstairs used to have the most glorious rows so we would hear all the language we never heard before. My mum would poke her head out the kitchen window and say, 'I think you'd better go in girls,' and we would say, 'No we're fine.' We would run upstairs, open our bedroom window and carry on listening. They would be throwing pots and pans at each other and the dinner would fly out the back door. We loved every minute of it.

When we did get a phone, we got a party line. My dad needed it for his work especially on Sunday night because he worked as a barrister's clerk and the briefs wanted to know what court they were in the next day. The woman we shared the line with was always on the phone. One Sunday evening my dad picked up the phone and she was talking away for ages so he said, 'Get off that phone or I'm coming round there. I know where you live.' We lost the party line pretty quick after that.

Roger Rogowski:

My mum was a full-time housewife and that was made possible in our house as my dad had two jobs. There was no washing machine, vacuum cleaner, fridge or dishwasher, so housework was more labour intensive then and my mum probably had it easier than most as there was only me to look after until my brother was born in 1959.

Until our first telly arrived, rented from the British Relay shop further along Kensal Road, the radio was our main contact with the outside world. Heavy and wooden like the old furniture, it lit up when switched on. Choices included the Light Programme and the Home Service and, more exotically, Hilversum and Luxembourg. One of my very early memories is that, whenever the 'Carousel Waltz' came on the radio, I would pester my mum to pick me up and whirl me round like a human carousel, which shows that the front room was big enough to swing a small child, never mind a cat.

After our telly arrived just before the 1962 Cup Final, it played a major part in home life after that. *Robin Hood*, *William Tell*, *Danger Man*, *Doctor Who* and, slightly later, *The Avengers*, and *The Prisoner* kept me captivated and *Ready Steady Go*, *Thank Your Lucky Stars* and *Juke Box Jury* heralded things to come for me. All the big news events of the time were shown right in our front room for the first time – the Cuban Missile Crisis, the Kennedy assassination and the first men in space – but my 10-year-old self could never understand what Christine Keeler and Mandy Rice-Davies were supposed to have done or why John Profumo had to resign no matter how many times they talked about it. Our living room door was unlocked during the day and one of the other children in the house, probably attracted by the sound of our new telly, opened the door one day to have a look and I'm sorry to say I punched him in the face and got into trouble.

In the summer, the air indoors could be stifling. The milk curdled even though it was delivered every day and the bottles were placed in the kitchen sink filled with cold water. Flies and bluebottles were always buzzing round in the summer and, even now, fly spray is a smell from those days. Right from when my nan was alive and for years after she died until we left Kensal Road, we would often spend Sunday afternoons at my nan and grandad's house. This meant taking the Metropolitan Line train from Westbourne Park to Hammersmith to change to the Piccadilly Line to Northfields. My stepbrother Alan, from my mum's first marriage, lived with them so he was a semi-detached part of our family. My grandparents had a spare bedroom, whereas we only had one bedroom for three of us and, later four when my younger brother was born.

We would usually travel over to see them after Sunday lunch, or dinner as we called it, and have tea with them in the afternoon. Dad was a bit disgusted with this English tradition, which usually consisted of cucumber sandwiches, watercress and Battenberg and iced fairy cakes, and he would often bring a supply of sausages or ham with him. In the days before our first telly arrived, it was a rare opportunity for us to do some viewing and our visit was always rounded off watching *Sunday Night at the London Palladium*, although it always looked like it was being performed in a fog on their ancient telly with its tiny screen set in a heavy wooden cabinet.

The only other family members to loom large were my mum's sister, Olive and her husband John. Childless, Olive was a secretary and John was a ground crew supervisor for BOAC at what was still called London Airport. They had all the trappings of pioneer yuppies, living in a detached bungalow in Greenford, owning a car and taking foreign holidays subsidised by BOAC, and they would visit us in Kensal Road from time to time barely hiding their disgust at where we lived, like Mr and Mrs Bouquet from *Keeping up Appearances*.

Bob Crawley:

There was no bathroom and bath time for the family was Sunday evening in a tin bath that was filled with water boiled on the gas cooker. As might be expected, the bath was small and the water shallow, and being the youngest child I had the first bath, which was normally too hot. Bath time was very quick with mum rubbing you very briskly with a flannel and Lifebuoy soap so that, even if you came out of the bath not 100 per cent clean, your skin glowed red from the effect of hot water and a roughly applied flannel and a bit of mum's spit for the ground-in areas of dirt. My parents used the tin bath after we had been put to bed but they also had use of my grandparents' bath at their house around the corner. It was a proper-size bath that was located in the kitchen and it had a hinged top that doubled up as the kitchen table.

Both rooms were lit by 60w bulbs but the landing still had gas lamps with a gauze-type covering. Prior to electric lights becoming standard, my uncle supposedly wired up an unofficial light from a street light outside but that stopped after the electricity company found out. Whether this was fact or myth, I don't know but I did hear the story on more than one occasion. As with many houses with shared occupancy, each floor had its own gas meter that took shillings and two bob pieces to keep the power on. The upside was that when the gas man came to empty the meters, each family got a cashback after the money had been counted and this was a bonus as money was always tight. The downside to cash meters was that they were frequently robbed as they were always located on open landings that many people could access. If the meter money was stolen, the affected family were held accountable and had to replace it. My mum hated paraffin heaters and wouldn't have one in the house because she said they were dangerous.

Our two rooms didn't have any form of heating in them but I don't recall ever being cold. That said, bedtime was strictly adhered to and was very early for children. The bedroom's sole use was for sleeping and it was never used for play or any other purpose. The kitchen had a rented TV that had two channels, BBC and ITV, and two radio stations, Home and Light Service. TV was just black and white and didn't start programmes until about four. *Robin Hood*, *William Tell*, *The Lone Ranger* and *Twizzle* were my favourite programmes.

In the last week of our stay in Golborne Gardens, my dad was offered some racing pigeons if he was prepared to kill them. That week we had pigeon on more than one occasion, although they were small. We moved to a flat, 17 Bramley House in Bramley Road, in about 1961, where my sister and I attended Thomas Jones School. Despite the flat in Bramley House having a proper kitchen, bathroom and three bedrooms, we continued to live to some extent as though still living in two rooms. My dad still shaved in the kitchen and the bathroom was used sparingly for bathing as the old one bath a week rule stayed in place, partly I think to my mum's fear of unaffordable gas and electricity bills and a general belief that no one needed more than one bath a week. Although Bramley Road was no more than a thirty-minute walk to my school in Bosworth Road, it was made clear to us children that we would move back to the old area as soon as a new flat became available.

A two-storey flat in Bosworth House became available in 1963, which was lovely: three bedrooms, kitchen, bathroom and downstairs toilet. I returned to St Andrew's School and we were back in the midst of our quite large extended family, probably twenty-five uncles, aunts, grandparents and cousins all within half a mile radius.

Christine Smith:

At Christmas, we had three days of parties at my gran's house. Christmas Eve was the children's party for us kids and our cousins who came down from Liverpool. Christmas Day was a family party and then Boxing Day was for all my aunts and uncles, friends and relations. Large barrels were obtained for liquid refreshment and the neighbours used to dance in their houses to the music they could hear coming through the walls from our parties, that is if they weren't invited in.

Brian Collins:

I was the second eldest. I had an older brother, then a younger brother, Chris. Then I had two sisters. We came in from school at different times so we never sat down together for tea. When we moved to the ground floor, because we had the lodger upstairs, for years I shared a bed with my older brother in the living room. If my Aunt Sally from Southam Street or my Auntie Anne from Fernhead Road were visiting, my parents would say 'It's time to go' when it was my bedtime, then they would open out the settee and my mum would get some sheets and a blanket from a cupboard and make the bed up, and that's how I slept until I was about 10. My sisters shared bunk beds and my two brothers Chris and Vincent slept in bunk beds.

We had a yard at the back of our house, so my dad thought he would put a bath up and it was the most primitive thing. It was a small bath filled by an Ascot with a long tube coming from the scullery. My dad was a hoarder and would never throw anything out, so there was a board on the top of the bath with half a ton of stuff on it. When I was 15 and wanted to start dating girls I said, 'I can't even have a bath in the house,' but on Saturday night, because we were going to church the next day, all the paint tins and other stuff on top of the bath would come off and we would have a bath. I shared a bath with my two brothers and my sisters would share a bath.

♯♭ Susan Mcmahon:

My mum worked really hard. She cooked us proper dinners every day except Fridays, when we had fish and chips or chicken and chips. Some of my friends would only have something like beans on toast. We all ate together. When my dad came in from work, it was dinner time.

four

Down our Street

∾ *Frank Hale:*

It was an area that was changing. Middle-class people were moving out and working-class people were moving in. There were still remnants of the old middle class. Opposite us were the Heffernans, who were concert pianists. Next to them lived Ken Richmond, the wrestler. He was famous as the man who banged the gong at the start of J. Arthur Rank films. The likes of the Heffernans were the last of the middle-class people. We were the rough people moving in.

Next door to the synagogue in Kensington Park Road was a sweet shop, which is now an Italian restaurant. The house was owned by an Italian family called Calliendo and it's still owned by the same family. Mr Calliendo took an English name and called himself Mr Thomas. He was interned in the Scrubs as an enemy alien at the start of the war and he was released when Italy surrendered.

When Convent Gardens was bombed in the war, the convent was damaged as well. After the war, there were seven houses left in Convent Gardens with Darkin's garage on the corner and three lock-up garages where the Belchers, the Kirks and the Cains used to store their barrows for the market, all well-known market families. I used to do odd jobs for them helping pull the barrows in and out. They would give me a shilling for doing that. The bombed houses in Convent Gardens were cleared and the ground was levelled off after the war and they put a boxing ring in one of the remaining houses, where I was taught to box. The *News of the World* came down and took some pictures of it in about 1948 or 1949.

In the 1950s, two families almost ran Notting Hill. The nephew of one family lived opposite me and we used to babysit for them and they would give us five bob for doing that, which was a lot of money then. They were like the Krays of the area. Their dad was serving a twelve-year stretch for armed robbery but they were very nice people, very well spoken. They were like gentlemen, not at all like ruffians. The family lived in a posh house further up the hill. They had a betting shop in Westbourne Park Road with the windows all blacked out. You could place a bet in there when it was illegal and the only way you could place a bet was in the street with the bookies' runners. Shows how powerful they were. When the police raided their betting shop in 1950, the *News of the World* got wind of it and it was all over the front page. There was another family. There were eleven of them and only one of them didn't go to prison at one time or another. They were up to all sorts. There were criminal groups but they never touched their own kind.

Con Cullen (left) and Roger Rogowski in Kensal Road, 1955, roughly where the north-east corner of Trellick Tower now stands. The only faintly recognisable landmarks are indicated by the patch of sunlight on the left where Golborne Road joins Kensal Road and the distant chimney, which still stands today.

What was Kensal Road and is now Elkstone Road, from the junction with Great Western Road, 1967. Modena Street is on the right and Southam Street further on, on the left, but only the brick wall on the extreme left remains.

✿ Jean Russell (née Hemming):

When I lived in Beethoven Street, everyone knew everyone else. Our mums would make sure the door knocker was Brasso'd and our steps were clean and our curtains were clean. I lived opposite Beethoven Street School. My mum would say, 'Don't go over the Town because they're rough.' She used to say there was a queen of the townies and the men used to carry her around and that she carried razors and had blades sewn in her clothes. We had a big air-raid shelter made from big breeze blocks outside our house in the road. There was a big pole in the corner of the shelter. I remember my dad carrying me into the shelter. My grandad had a shelter in the garden with a big mound on top with flowers. We played in the shelter for years after the war. We would all get in the shelter and giggle. There was all bunk beds inside.

My brother-in-law, Len, came home after the war. He didn't want to go back in the army. He came from a big family. His mum had twenty-one children and lost fourteen of them, a lot of them with pneumonia. He was a coalman driving a horse and cart before the war. He got my sister pregnant when he was 16 and she was 15. It was an absolute scandal and my mum kept the child and brought her up for two years. She always believed her mum and dad had a different wedding date, so she was lied to most of her life. Len wanted to get out of the army so he went in the shelter and the men from the street, including my uncles and my dad, got this big metal pipe and used it to get one of the breeze blocks out of the wall and they dropped it on his leg and broke it to get him out of the army because his leg was in plaster. The kids were all watching while they were doing it.

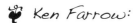 Ken Farrow:

There was Shaw's sweet shop, which was the second shop from the corner of Kensal Place and Edenham Street, with the shoe factory shop on the corner. There was another kind of factory shop on the corner of Kensal Road and Kensal Place. These shops had sheets or curtains across the windows so you couldn't see in. A few of them were distribution places for home workers, like making jewellery. They would take the parts home and put them together and get paid something like a shilling for putting a hundred of something together, terrible rates but a way of making a few bob.

There was the stationer's we called the 'white shop' in Golborne Road, then there was Wardale's the sweet shop and tobacconist. A woman, her sister and her husband ran the shop, then there was the greengrocer's, then the post office on the corner of Golborne Road and Edenham Street. On the other corner of Golborne Road and Edenham Street was another factory shop, then Mr Wilkinson's sweet shop. He had a private library where you could pay him a penny to borrow a book for a week. My mum used to read all his books and wait for him to get new ones in. When he closed his shop before they built Trellick, he went to work in Selfridges. I later found out he was a master tailor.

After that was Mrs Martin's shop, then her husband Mr Martin's, which we called the 'green shop'. We only went in there for cold meats. We went into Blood's in Adair Road for our main items during the week. When we moved to Kensal Road, we used Batchelor's in Kensal Road past Kensal Place near Kew's, which sold veggies and flowers. If they were closed, we would go to Pamphlion's on the corner of Kensal Place and Southam Street opposite Craven House. Davis' dairy was next in Golborne Road after the green shop, then Bowen's the chemist, then the bagwash. You would take your laundry along in a bag and they would wash it in the bag. We took it round on a pram because there was so many of us at home. It was like it weighed a hundredweight and coming back it was even heavier when it was wet and you had to dry it at home.

✣ Jane Traies:

When I went to Wornington Road Infants, I would walk up Chesterton Road on my own and I would go in to see my granny and grandad in Golborne Road, so they knew I'd got that far, then I would go on to school. On the corner of Wornington by the Mitre, there would be a lovely old carthorse eating from his black greasy nosebag.

St Michael's Church in Ladbroke Grove was our social life for quite a long time. It was a tradition that you got your kids out of the house on a Sunday so you could have five minutes to yourself. St Michael's was Anglo-Catholic. Although our parents were believers, they weren't high church at all. They didn't do the smells and bells. Dad came from a chapel-going family but St Michael's was on the next corner, so we received all this high Christianity, which wasn't what our parents believed at all.

No. 100 Golborne, where my granny and grandad lived, backed onto Munro Mews and all those houses had a back door onto the Mews. My grandad would take me up the Mews to see the horses. The yellow horse piss would be running between the cobbles. In between the stables, there were the tic tac men with the runner on the corner. That was when betting wasn't legal. Our grandad was a great one for a bet.

In Mum's day, when she was a young girl, she used to go to the Golborne Road chapel when it was a chapel in the 1920s. She said she used to watch magic lantern shows in there and, after they showed them, you had to say if you'd been saved. We used to call it the nick because the Reverend Peake used to look after ex-prisoners there.

There was a bagwash at the top of Ladbroke Grove up by the Admiral Blake. When I was at Barlby, my friends would sometimes say after school,

'I've got to go and collect my mum's bagwash,' and I didn't understand what a bagwash was for a long time. It was pre-launderette days. You put all your washing in a bag and took it in. I remember the first black child I ever saw in Ladbroke Grove was a little girl about my own age, because there were very few families then. Her name was Josie. They were mostly working men but, within a few years of that, there was a really mixed community.

Margaret Burdsey (née Traies):

On the corner of Chesterton Road and Portobello Road, there was the post office and I was always fascinated that, because there was a huge Irish Catholic community in the area, there were rosaries, icons and triptych things in the window.

There were nuns at St Michael's church, which was our local church going north along Ladbroke Grove. Our social life as we were growing up in the Fifties and Sixties revolved around that church because we went to the Brownies there. When we first went, Brownie meetings were in the church hall in Bonchurch Road on Wednesday nights. Our Brown Owl knew someone who produced plays, so we put on the most magnificent nativity plays in the church hall and then in St Michael's church. Because Jane and I were always good at remembering words, we always had speaking parts rather than being singing angels, parts like small shepherd, older shepherd, King Herod, and my brother John was one of my slaves one year. Colin Brown, the son of the local bookmaker, started eating the incense one year. He thought it was sweets.

I was 5½ when John was born and I used to push him in his pram up Ladbroke Grove as far as the bridge to look at the trains when he was sitting up and taking notice. He was a daisy boy when he was older for the church's patronal festival at St Michael and All Angels in Ladbroke Grove. When we had a service and paraded round the church, the servers carried bunches of Michaelmas daisies. Later, he served at the altar for some services at St Mark's Church in the mid-Sixties, mainly eight o'clock communion, for Father John Armson. When he was about 12, we used to walk up the lane on a Saturday morning to Notting Hill Gate and treat him to a cup of coffee and we thought that was special.

There was a street cleaner who mainly pushed his barrow around Chesterton Road, Golborne Road and St Charles' Square and he was obviously a very damaged person. Maybe he'd been damaged in the war. He used to talk to himself and shout at people. We were terrified of him as children. We called him Pompom Joe because of his hat. He would shout things like, 'Do you want the job or don't you?' He terrified us.

We used to love to see the horse artillery towing the cannons down Chesterton Road on their way to the Scrubs. Our Uncle Georgy used to run outside with a bucket to pick up the horse dung as soon as they went past. The only time we went over the iron bridge in Golborne Road, when Jane and I were very little, was to see Doctor Ross. In a way he was like a caricature out of a film because he was Scottish, he had ginger hair and he had half glasses on his nose. His surgery was in an old corner shop on the corner of Golborne and Appleford. It was bare wooden benches in what used to be the shop where you waited in order to be seen. He was one of those pioneer NHS doctors who worked in the slums. It was such a thing that he would come to our house and when he did, Mum would always put a clean apron on and call him doctor.

I remember Richard Burton being filmed in the Elgin for *The Spy who Came in From the Cold*. They shot the scene several times and it was supposed to be raining, so they kept spraying him with water every time before he walked in the pub. It was on a Sunday afternoon, so there was a crowd of people watching what was going on.

John Traies:

There was always a bonfire on the corner of St Lawrence Terrace in the road on bonfire night. They would build up the pile for the fire for days before bonfire night. There weren't that many cars in those days, so they would just drive round it on the pavement. The tarmac would begin to melt and eventually you would hear the fire engine coming to put it out. They would have a bonfire in Munro Mews and throw jumping jacks into the fire and they would be jumping all over the place. We had a penny for the guy pitch on the corner of St Lawrence Terrace by the postbox. The guy used to sit in my go-kart, which I called Thunderflash.

The Percy was run by an Irishman called Higgins. At Christmas, you couldn't see across the bar they had so many decorations hanging across the ceiling. There was always a fight every Saturday night. They shot a few scenes for *Z Cars* outside our shop. They would pay Dad a fiver because no one else could use the machines while they were filming. Someone like Bert Lynch would get out the car and buy a pack of cigarettes. Just along Ladbroke Grove past the railway bridge, there was the dentist that I used to go to. They used to gas you and you could hear the loud noise from those old-fashioned drills while you were waiting to go in. The anaesthetic was so slow you had to go back and sit in the waiting room until it worked.

My dad was the only parent who had a car so, if he drove it to school sometimes, my friends would say, 'Mr Traies can we have a drive round the block in your car?' so he would load about six kids in the car and drive along Wheatstone Road and along Golborne to Wornington. It was a Ford Consul 375. There was a family of eight across the road from us in Bevington Road when we lived in Golborne Road and some of them didn't have shoes on.

🌿 *Pauline Clark (née Harding):*

We lived opposite the Catholic church in Bosworth Road and used to see all the weddings, funerals and christenings. Father used to say people go in to have their sins forgiven then come out and go in the club next door, get drunk, come out swearing, then want to be forgiven again. Dad was a Catholic but we were brought up C of E.

The Grand Union Canal was just round the corner. There was always someone falling in that couldn't swim. Round by the ha'penny steps was the swimming baths. I could swim at 5. We had swimming every week at school. There was also a place in the baths where mothers could do their washing and anyone could have a bath.

If you wanted to make a phone call, you had to go up to the post office to make the call. If you wanted to have a bet on a horse or a pigeon race, there would be a man standing in a doorway called a runner. He would take the bet as it wasn't legal in those days. When I was 5, I was run over crossing Kensal Road getting a paper for an 83-year-old. I spent a month in hospital. Sweets had to be handed in and a nurse would come round with a plate of sweets and you could choose two.

 *Dennis Smith:*

I would go round to the playground in Kensal House. I would be in the playground playing football and the caretaker would see me and say 'Out' because only kids who lived in Kensal House were allowed to play there.

I used to go and get coke out of the gasworks. I would get an old pram and fill it with bags at a shilling a bag. I used to go fishing in the canal and I saw all this coke piled 50 foot up and it never seemed to be getting used so I thought, 'Why am I buying it?' The gasworks were open to sell coke on Wednesdays and Saturdays, so we would go on Tuesday nights and Friday nights. There was a gate in Ladbroke Grove but it was never open so we had to climb over the bridge with the pram across two big pipes, climb over the wall and fill about ten or fifteen bags up and save all that money. I had to walk all the way to the Scrubs pushing the pram loaded up and all the way back to Ladbroke Grove. I'd sell them for a shilling a bag. That was a bleeding lot of money.

I used to collect newspapers and take them to the fish and chip shop and get a bag of chips for them. They only wanted clean newspapers so I would go round taking the papers they put in the letterboxes. We'd go to Kensington Gardens and go round people collecting the empty Coke bottles asking, 'Have you finished with that?' and get tuppence back on the bottle. We used to go to the Essoldo cinema in Great Western Road or the Prince of Wales in Harrow Road. One of us would pay to go in and, when it was dark, go and open the door up and let the others in.

I used to smoke and still do. One day, when I was about 13 or 14, I was standing at the bottom of the block having a fag when someone came down and put their rubbish out. It was my friend Johnny Kingsbury's mum. She said, 'You don't go around with my John no more.' I thought I'd better not say nothing because he used to come down and have a smoke with me. I said to him later, 'Your mum caught me smoking.' He said she put her hand in his pockets and found a packet of ten Guards. He said, 'I told her they were yours and I was looking after them for you.' You could buy four Dominos in a packet for sixpence or there was tuppenny loose.

The bloke downstairs from us used to keep his bike outside and one day we thought we would take it so we tied a hook on a clothes line and started to pull the bike up. We got it 4 foot from us and the bike got caught. We kept on pulling and half our balcony gave way and fell down with the bike. We had to put a plank across afterwards to get to the lavatory. There was a family lived in Edenham Street near the Seven Feathers. They were a family. One time they offered to babysit for a couple of hours for two bob while this lady went shopping and when she come back, the gas meter had been done and the babysitter had gone.

 ## Derek Ford:

We lived three or four doors from the Earl Percy, opposite St Charles' Square where the 52 bus used to turn round. The No. 15s used to turn round by the Eagle in Telford Road. The church in St Charles' Square was Catholic and the Percy was full of Irish people. They would congregate outside around ten on Sunday morning. Obviously the pub wasn't open. They would play penny up the wall until eleven or eleven thirty, then they would go in for their Mass and would come out and go in the pub. When they came out the pub, there was fights galore every Sunday. We would look out for them.

In my early years from age 5 to 10, we were in Kensal Road regular from Chesterton Road because my grandmother's sister, Rose Grimmer, lived in Southern Row. She was previously Rose Hoare. She divorced from her husband, Alfie Hoare, and he moved to Kensal Road near Wedlake Baths. I used to go to the baths sometimes. I spent a lot of time visiting my nan and grandad. I don't remember anything that was fearful for me. When I got rid of my three-wheeler, I had a bike and I used to cycle all round the streets. I would stay out late and, when I got home, there would be Dad at the window shouting, 'Get in here.' The only street I was wary of was Southam Street. One day, coming back from my nan's house in Southern Row to come over the Golborne Road bridge, I saw this massive crowd and there was these two blokes fighting in the middle of the road. They had their shirts off and they were covered in blood and I always avoided that street after that. I must have been 8 or 9 at the most.

In the school holidays we would collect all the old rags and newspapers we could find and take them to an old boy in Bevington Road. He would only give us tuppence or threepence for them. We would also take him old soda bottles and he would give us a couple of pence. He was a massive old boy. He would throw the rags and papers on these old scales. Being a little kid, I was a bit wary of him but when I got out outside, plus what I scrounged off my brother, because he was six years older, and my nan and my grandad, I had a nice amount.

❧ Richard Rowlands:

I remember the first betting shop in Adair Road. Akers. He used to run it. Before that, this big ginger bloke used to stand on the corner. He was the bookie's runner. It was hard round here then. My dad come up and there was these two blokes having a fight outside the pub and one of them knocked the other bloke out so he said to him, 'You've had enough,' but the other bloke came back and said, 'You want some?' so my dad beat him up because the bloke was the local bully. They come for my dad the next day but he beat the both of them.

❁ Gwen Nelson (née Martin):

Few people owned cars in North Kensington. The few vehicles we did see were the totters' ponies and carts, the milk cart, men cycling to work or delivery vans. Twice a week there was excitement in the form of the King's Troop clattering along Golborne Road on its way from the barracks in St John's Wood to Wormwood Scrubs where they performed manoeuvres and exercises with their guns. Following in their wake were locals with buckets and shovels to scoop up the horses' droppings because it was good manure.

Next door to us at 19 were an elderly couple, Bert and Amy Cross, who were originally from Earls Barton in Northamptonshire. He had been an apprentice at Clark's shoe makers as a young man and was operating as a snob, as shoe makers were known in those days. In 1959 he decided to retire and the shop came up for lease. As I was now at grammar school and there was a limit to how much Mum could do in my father's shop, my parents decided to lease No. 19 and Mum was going to run it as a drapers, ladies' clothing and wool shop, since the closest one was the other end of Golborne Road, over the iron bridge.

Along our side of Golborne Road, just down from the corner with Kensal Road was a stationer's that sold all sorts of types of paper, bond, antique laid, kraft, Manilla and vellum. Next door was a sweetshop, Wardale's, run by an old woman who was always knitting. A girl about my age, Gillian, lived with her but I'm not sure of their relationship. Sweets were displayed on an open counter for you to choose your own mixture. A friend and I would go in and ask the woman the time. To tell us, she had to go out the back to see the clock and in her absence we'd stuff as many sweets as we could into our pockets. We were never caught but I'm sure she must have suspected. Gillian was a plump child with golden ringlets and elaborate, hand-knitted, lacy dresses. For some reason she never fitted in with the other children on the street and we'd tease her by tugging her hair.

On the corner of Golborne and Edenham was a post office and across Edenham Street lived Mrs Mabley with her children. I was friends for a short while with Ann Mabley and we would go to the Saturday morning Minors at the Prince of Wales cinema on Harrow Road. I don't recall there being a Mr Mabley. No. 15 was a tobacconist and sweet shop run by the Whites, who had two sons, Gordon and Raymond, about my age. Raymond had a bit of a crush on me and would sneak sweets to me when his dad wasn't looking. No. 17 Golborne was also a shop. Its function varied as no one ever seemed to make a go of it. The only business I can recall being there for any length of time was a second-hand shop that sold reconditioned electrical goods. No. 19 was the premises of the shoe repairer Bert Cross and his wife, Amy. They were unusual in that they were a childless couple and had the whole property to themselves.

The other side of us, No. 23, held three families, all of whom were immigrants. The Gonzalez and Ramayons were Spanish and the Christous were Greek Cypriot. The Christis' daughter, Yiannoula, was my best friend and partner in shoplifting. There was a dairy at 27 run by a Welshman, Dai Francis. His daughter married Kenny Ball's bassist Vic Pitt and, on a couple of occasions, gave us tickets for a Kenny Ball concert. There was a friendly agreement between Dai and my dad that Dad wouldn't sell fresh milk and Dai wouldn't sell meat or bacon, although Dad did sell sterilised milk. As many people didn't have a refrigerator, it had the advantage of lasting longer than regular milk.

Further along was a chemist, Bowen's, run by an older man and his son. The bagwash was on the corner of our block going towards the iron bridge. The iron bridge crossed over the railway line and was frequently adorned with four-letter words. I was a precocious reader and proud of my skill. On one occasion when walking across the bridge with Mum, I saw the letters F-U-C-K. Eager to show how clever I was I said loudly to Mum, 'Look Mummy, F-U-C-K, that spells fuck.' The more she shushed me, the more I said it until well across the bridge, not that my use of the word would have raised many eyebrows on Golborne Road. It was common parlance and children were often addressed as 'you little fucker' as a term of endearment. The 'C word' was also used as an everyday term.

Across the road, at the Kensal Road end, were several shops. One was a fish and chip shop but the proprietors were very surly and expected you to bring your own newspaper in which to wrap the fish and chips. We always preferred the Greek shop the other side of the iron bridge. On the corner of Hazlewood Crescent was the Prince Arthur pub. During the week it was pretty quiet but Friday and Saturday nights, it was regularly the scene of fights. It was not only men who indulged in fisticuffs but women, particularly the local toms who had fallen out over a client. They would strip off to the waist and bare-knuckle box, pull hair and claw at each other until either other customers or the police broke them up. Most Fridays and Saturdays the Black Maria would arrive and the miscreants bundled in and taken down to Harrow Road police station. This was weekend entertainment from the balcony seats of our first-floor lounge. Mum and Dad always said it was better than what was on our 9-inch black and white telly.

One evening in the late 1950s, *Sanders of the River* was on the telly and there was a full-on racial conflict raging outside the pub. During the race riots, men would pull up the iron railings and charge each other. The same thing was happening on TV with assegais. As Dad said, 'On TV it was blacks chasing whites with spears and downstairs it was whites chasing blacks with spears!'

No. 20 on the corner with Appleford Road was a doctor's surgery at ground level and lodgings for several single men on the upper floors. The Powers who lived in the basement were Irish. Mrs Power was the doctor's housekeeper and their daughter Kayleen was also one of my friends. The other side of Appleford Road was a closed shop that was used as a workshop by a bespoke tailor. Above it lived a couple who I think were Polish with a daughter, Juleika. Juleika and I were friends until one day she refused to return a book I had lent her. It was a very old one about cats illustrated by Louis Wain and one of my favourites. I came home wailing and Dad went over to see her mum but was told she wouldn't make Juleika hand it back as, 'Gwen has so much and Juleika has so little.' I never spoke to her again.

In Hazlewood Crescent, behind Hazlewood Tower, was a mews with stabling for the totters' horses and lock-ups to store their carts and goods. I became friendly with one of the totters and, horse mad from a young age, I would hang around after school, waiting for them to return from a day's collecting. I'd help unharness the pony, groom him, feed him and clean his harness. This was six days a week and on Sunday, their day off,

I'd be rewarded for my work by being allowed to ride up and down the cobblestone mews for about half an hour.

 ## Jeannie Rowe (née Searson):

Very occasionally we went down to Latimer Road Baths, where there were public baths. You hired a bathroom. I always remember the beautifully polished copper taps and pipes, and then you had a proper bath. We also used to go swimming there. We had to walk past the end of Rillington Place to get there. That always produced a certain frisson because, as young as we were, we knew of its reputation.

Charlie Phillips:

Regardless of the racial barriers, it was a close-knit community. I saw racism from both sides. I saw racism against the Irish. When I came here there was a big influx of Hungarians as well. In my school, there was kids who couldn't even speak English and they often got attacked. Some kids came from a racist family. When they couldn't pick on me, they would pick on the Irish kids and call them Spud Murphy and Potato Paddy. Kids are kids but I used to get harassed by the elder teddy boys. I got attacked once by some teddy boys and this English woman came out and said, 'Leave him alone. Leave that coloured boy alone.'

In 1958, I used to be an altar boy, the first coloured altar boy at St Michael's. A lot of us came from a strong religious background. I used to have to help out in the church because the family needs a bit of space on Sunday. I used to go to church at seven o'clock, have a bit of breakfast in the vicarage, go to St Michael's at nine o'clock and do the big one at eleven o'clock.

There was this man. He was in the air force and he stayed after the war and he picked up this house for £400 in Blenheim Crescent. It was very easy after the war to buy property and that's how Rachman got his properties. Some of these houses went for £500 and you would pay £7 a week if you could get a loan. My friend Alan used to live above a fruit and veg shop on the corner of Westbourne Park Road and All Saints Road. His dad paid £450 for that shop in 1954. Later on, Alan turned it into a second-hand furniture shop, bric-a-brac and all that, and he used to participate in carnivals selling soft drinks, Coca Cola and all that.

The communal meeting place was Lancaster Road public baths on a Saturday morning, where people would be there doing their laundry. In some of the houses they never had bathrooms and a lot of houses had toilets in the backyards, especially Tavistock Road.

When I was a child, there was a lady who was a regular in the fish and chip shop in Ladbroke Grove. She had grey hair but she looked Spanish. She was the first one to give me a thick ear. If we didn't have much money, we used to buy crackling. Nowadays they can't sell it any more because of health and safety. I was coming home from school and I must have broken the queue because she went 'pow' round my head and told me to get back in the queue. George's in Portobello Road, just before you reach the bridge, was my regular greasy spoon. They were a Greek family. Opposite was Steve, another Greek, who also ran a greasy spoon. If my parents were coming home late I would go in there and have egg, chips and peas for one and six until they come home.

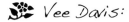 *Vee Davis:*

The Tabernacle was where I come to church. When I first come, I come to the church here. All of us come in our pyjamas and your overcoat over you and you come to church. The major thing with us in those days, coming out to say like you're going to a church just to keep warm, you have to burn the paraffin in the house. You know the Electric Cinema. That was the bug house. You pay whatever and you go in there and you keep warm for an hour and a half and you see a film, so going to places like that is to keep warm because you had to buy the paraffin and everything and you all smell of paraffin.

Margaret Stedman (née Riddick):

My dad loved a drink. One day, he took me out in the pushchair. I must have been 18 months or 2 years old. He walked me up Carlton Hill to the Carlton Bridge Tavern, had a few drinks, came out the pub and started to walk down Kensal Road and got arrested for being drunk in charge of a pushchair. He got taken to Harrow Road police station. They didn't charge him because they thought, when they walked him back home, knocking on the front door and having to face my mum would be punishment enough.

The lady who ran the RSPCA in Kensal Road lived next door to us. I'd grazed my knee in the street one day and there was no one at home as my mum was out at work. The lady picked me up out the street and took me in to her house. While she was bathing my leg, I spotted this square tray in the corner and said, 'What's that?' She said, 'It's a shower,' and I said, 'What does that do?' I said to my mum later, 'They've got something called a shower.'

My nan worked at BDH and forced me to take vitamin capsules because she got them free at work, or maybe she only said she got them free, who knows? She lived in one of the small houses that are still there in Middle Row. That belonged to White Knight, just down from the Lads of the Village. It had a bedroom, kitchen, lounge and a bathroom with a half bath. There was a sweet shop in Kensal Place run by a huge woman we always called fat Ada but never to her face. Going up to Carlton bridge on the corner of Kensal Place was a bubblegum factory and there was always a sweet sickly smell around there. I remember the Littles across the road from us, Fred and Pat and their daughter, Jean. She was the first one with a record player so she was my best friend. Pat Little worked in White Knight until she retired. The area had a reputation. Later, when I had boyfriends, I didn't want them to see where I lived so I would say to them, 'Just drop me at the station and I can make my own way back.'

❈ Ray Matthews:

Nan, who was my dad's mother, was a gypsy and such a character, always betting on horses. I had to take her bets round to a pub near Fowell Street, give the bet to the runner who was outside and just walk on. She didn't often win but every Monday morning my grandad's suit went in the pawn shop. She would say to me, ''Ere son, do me a favour, pop this round to uncle's.' Uncle's was Bosher's the pawn shop by Latimer Road station. It gave my nan a couple of bob to bet with. When Grandad gave my nan her wages as she called it Friday afternoon, I had to run round to Bosher's and get his suit back as every man wore a suit on the weekend back then.

Another thing that springs to mind is collecting jam jars and beer bottles to take back to Jim's in Mary Place to get money back on the jam jars or beer bottles back to the off-licence, then nipping in to Mrs Thomas's shop in Mortimer Square for a penny drink and a tuppeny loose. A lot of people come round the streets selling. The winkle man called round every Sunday, the man selling toffee apples, the man on his three-wheeled bike sharpening knives, the corner man every Thursday and the baker in his van calling nearly every day with fresh bread.

I remember the awful fogs when you literally couldn't see your hand in front of your face and sitting by the fire having toast after getting out of the tin bath on a Sunday evening while listening to Dan Dare on the radio. When I was 10, I was allowed to go for a bath instead of the tin bath in the kitchen. You paid a few pence and could stay for ages, even calling out to the bloke who put the water in, 'More hot No. 5,' or whatever number cubicle you were in.

Babs Coker:

I recall my dad running a betting book. He used to throw dice on street corners for money and always had a lookout in case the police came. I remember as a kid sitting outside the Eagle in Ladbroke Grove while my dad was inside drinking.

Reg Thackeray:

The church in Golborne Road was run by the Reverend Peake, who took in loads of ex-prisoners who had nowhere else to go. They lived upstairs in cubicles with a bed in each one and, one time, there was a fire and two of them got burned to death. There was Acorn Dairy owned by Mr and Mrs Cron. They sold it to move to Ramsgate to open a bed and breakfast and there was a fire in the flat upstairs and two people burned to death. Paraffin heaters were responsible for a lot of fires. The drip-feed type heaters were the worst ones. There was a fire caused by a paraffin heater in St Ervans Road when I was a kid.

I remember some of the totters, Bobby King and Monty the deaf man. Some of them kept their horses and carts in the shed in the triangle in

Bevington Road and there were a lot of them down Latimer Road. You could buy good stuff from them. I think people were sympathetic for the horse and thought that, by giving something, they were helping to look after the horse. When my sister was young, there used to be a roundabout on a cart and, to get a ride, you had to give them clothing or a hat or jam jars. The totter used to wind the handle to make the roundabout go. Another one used to give you a goldfish. Children would take all sorts of things out just to get a go on the roundabout or get a goldfish and it sometimes used to cause an argument if they gave away something they shouldn't have. The totters would shout 'Rag bo, rag bo' when they went round the streets.

On Sunday, Mr Pratt, who only had a handcart, used to come round with shellfish, cockles, shrimps and whelks calling out and another man came round with a wooden fruit box with a rope round it off his shoulder filled with toffee apples for fourpence and bigger ones for sixpence shouting, 'Toffee app, toffee app 'ere.'

Your dad's suit would be used at the weekend and would be pawned on Monday at Cook's pawnshop. There were two pawnshops. One where the Lisboa is now and one next door. They had some really good unredeemed things in the window. The ladies would do the washing at Wedlake Street Baths. The sheets would be washed and ironed and they would go into pawn as well until you got your wages at the weekend and got them back.

🌿 Marg Pithers:

In Barlby Road we used to have the King's Troop come past our house on their way from their barracks to the big Scrubs. We would follow them down to see if there was any horseshoes. Some of them would tie their horses up at the bus stop on the way back while they went in and bought fags. One day, one set of horses must have been spooked because they charged down Barlby Road pulling a gun carriage twisted over with all sparks coming off the road.

🐦 Roger Rogowski:

Opposite our house at 89 Kensal Road was a mission hall, where I sometimes went to Sunday school, although I preferred Saturday mornings at the

Essoldo in Great Western Road. Next door but one to the chapel heading west was Knitmaster, a manufacturer of knitting machines housed in a large red brick building, which was a former United Dairies.

Further along, in a parade of shops facing the junction with Golborne Road, was a Greek Cypriot barber where I had my hair cut. When I was still too small for the barber's chair, he would produce a plank of wood and place it across the arms of the chair for me to sit on. Hair for men and boys was often cropped short almost up to the crown and, to do that, the barber used hand clippers, which must have had some teeth missing because he almost pulled as much hair out from the back of my head as he cut. In the same parade of shops was the British Relay shop, where my parents rented our telly, as they were still too expensive for many people to buy and, anyway, they were also very unreliable, breaking down on a regular basis. With a rented telly, it was the rental company's problem if it broke down.

There was an RSPCA surgery in a small parade of shops between our house and the junction with Golborne Road and a red phone box, which usually had a queue of people waiting their turn. I think everyone respected that people were waiting and each call never seemed to be long and, anyway, we could only ever call someone with a private phone, so calls were limited to my mum's parents and her sister. A betting shop was opened later along the same parade and I'm sure they did good business next door to the Britannia, a Truman's pub with a tiled exterior that stood on the corner of Kensal and Golborne Roads. It always seemed to be packed as I remember; if one of the doors was opened whenever I walked past, there was always a blast of noise mixed with the smell of stale beer and cigarette smoke. I bet it was good in there.

Beyond the junction with Golborne Road, on the left, there were a number of small businesses operating, one of which, Saga Records, pressed records. There were usually boxes of rejects outside, sometimes only rejected because they had the same label on both sides or the labels stuck on slightly off-centre. It was always a bit of a game to see how many records we could pick up and run off with before someone came out and tried to catch us but we were usually halfway down the road before they saw us. Also towards the Ladbroke Grove end of Kensal Road, Askey's wafer factory was a good source for free wafers. I'd assumed at the time that boxes of wafers were left outside for children to help themselves but I've since found out that, if we were helping ourselves, it wasn't because they were giving them away.

The concept of nicking seemed to be a bit of a grey area in those days. The ha'penny chews, fruit salads and black jacks, within easy reach at the front of the counter in sweet shops, were always fair game when the shopkeeper's back was turned while measuring out a quarter of sweets from a jar but bigger items could be risky. An enterprising school friend of mine supplemented his pocket money by stealing Matchbox toys to order from Woolworths in Harrow Road and selling them for half price. I also remember a coin-collecting school friend coming to school one Monday morning showing off a gold spade guinea from the reign of George III. He said he'd found it in the gutter in Portobello Road after the stallholders had left. I thought that was lucky but, looking back, maybe it was more than luck. Also along Kensal Road, on the corner of the road leading to the ha'penny steps, was the old swimming baths, which was always freezing and smelt so strongly of chlorine, my eyes were almost watering before I got in. It wasn't all bricks and tarmac as, at the junction of Kensal Road and East Row was, and still is, the little rec, which included a children's playground with swings, rocking horse, roundabout and witch's hat, and the beautifully landscaped Emslie Horniman Pleasance.

When I was older, my dad started giving me pocket money. He was paid monthly and thought I would learn to manage my money better if he paid me monthly too and so he gave me a pound a month. It was tricky to make sure the money didn't run out before the month and there was plenty of temptation to spend it. I got my sweets either from Wardale's, just round the corner in Golborne Road, or Ada Tyne's in Kensal Place. The Wardales were usually in their back room watching their telly, which was very high up and appeared to be on the top of a wardrobe facing the shop while they had their backs to the shop, so they weren't always that swift in coming into the shop to serve. Smaller sweets, like fruit salads and black jacks, which were on display at the front of the counter, were easy picking until one of the Wardales shuffled out to serve me, although I never took sweets from Ada's shop because, apart from being extremely big, she was a very scary woman.

My dad wanted me to save some pocket money and I usually managed to put a minimal amount into my savings book each month in the post office at the corner of Golborne Road and Edenham Street. Further down Golborne Road, on the left over the iron bridge, there was Harper's, which doubled as a toy and record shop, where I went from time to time to add to my Corgi car collection. Later on, it was in Harper's that I started my record collection. Singles cost 6s and 3d before going up to 6s and 8d, so that was a major investment out of my pocket money. Woolworths in Portobello Road sold cover versions of hit singles on their own Embassy label and these were cheaper but they were as bad as the records I occasionally liberated from the boxes outside Saga Records.

My mum was a regular in Vic Martin's grocer's shop in Golborne Road. I know that he was a serious stamp collector as he very generously gave me a large quantity of old British and Colonial stamps in a folder, which more than supplemented my meagre schoolboy-level collection. It was such a generous act that I often thought about why he would have done that. I will never know for sure but it's possible that, as my father lived in Silesia before the war, where Vic Martin was interned as a POW, they had that in common.

Mossy Condon:

We were backing onto the stables in the mews where they kept the horses. Opposite was a lady, Mrs Couch, who used to pick me up from school and look after me until after my mum finished work. One day we were swinging over an old basement in Edenham Street next to the post office and a black Zephyr pulled up. The driver stayed in the car and this guy ran out with a stocking on his head and a gun in his hand and he robbed the post office. The police came round what seemed like ages later and they asked us if we saw anything.

I remember one of the first ever carnivals. There were three lorries and we jumped on the back of one of them and they took us along Hazlewood Crescent and Golborne Road, and we jumped off at the Warwick because we thought they were taking us too far. There were steel bands playing off the back of them and it was a novelty to us. There were no stalls out until later on.

Barbara Reynolds (née Murray):

I had such a brilliant time. If I could go there tomorrow with everything that was there in my day, I would go back without a thought. It was a community. There was no locked doors. Everybody knew you so you never got in any trouble. They never had to worry about where you were. There was always someone about who knew your mum, knew your dad, knew your gran. You never thought, 'Don't talk to that man.' There was just complete trust.

Bob Crawley:

The houses in Golborne Gardens and surrounding streets were owned by numerous landlords and rented out. They were overcrowded and not fit for human occupation. Because the houses were in very poor condition, street by street was compulsorily purchased by the council and set for a major slum clearance programme, which resulted in many families becoming council tenants for the first time.

When we moved back to the area, because Bosworth House along with Appleford House were some of the earliest new flats, together with Adair and Hazlewood Towers, I was able to witness the demolition of the surrounding streets and play in the houses as they were vacated before demolition. The condemned houses also became useful to film and TV producers and it wasn't uncommon to come home from school and see films or TV programmes being made.

Tragedy seemed to occur on a regular basis and I lost two West Indian school friends, Lloyd and Ira Whatley, in a house fire caused by a paraffin heater. Paraffin heaters were very popular as they were cheap to buy and run, and people would move them around the house by picking them up, causing flames to spill out from the top. A lot of friends had them in their houses. I remember one fire caused by an upturned paraffin heater in Wheatstone Road and seeing fire engines outside while I was walking past to collect dog meat for my nan's dog. One of the kids from Bosworth House fell through the roof of the bus garage in Middle Row and a couple got killed in road accidents. A couple of my friends lost parents to cancer and I remember the fear that cancer could be caught from someone who had it.

Christine Smith:

There was only one set of parents who had a car in the whole time I was at St Mary's from 1960 to 1966 and they were the McManus family, who unusually for the time, had their mother drive them to school from Harlesden Gardens. We would run to the wire fencing to see them get in or out of their car. It was a huge status symbol to have a car in your family. We had an uncle, George, who lived next door to us and he was a black cab driver with his own taxi. At weekends he would take us out to see his friends in Pinner or Harrow and on a Saturday would take my sister and me to learn to swim at Porchester Street Baths. We were supposed to be learning at Wedlake Street but the woman who was the swimming teacher at the baths was always screaming at the children and running up and down the pool with a large pole and hoop. We were terrified of her and I didn't learn a stroke there.

I can remember there was a shop being used in Kensal Road for filming. I'm not sure what the film was but the shop was made out like a shop of easy virtue. Some of the mothers from the school went in and gave the person behind the counter hell saying that there were young kids going by and it was disgraceful. They didn't let the person behind the counter get a word in edgeways, only to find out it was a film set being made up before the cameras were there.

My best friend from secondary school, Margaret, lived in Swinbrook Road. I spent a large amount of time in the area as a teenager. We used to watch the carnival, which was a very small affair in those days, nothing to what it has become now. Margaret and I also watched during the time Trellick Tower was being built and the Westway. Trellick Tower became a place no one wanted to live because it was vandalised so much. The lifts were always out of order and I remember one Christmas where, for about four days, the residents had no heating or lifts working and they had had a dreadful time. The Westway had a huge impact on the area. We hated the concrete under-carriageways and how it just cut through so much of the area and we were told what progress was being made. We spent a lot of time in Portobello Road, which was becoming trendy in the Sixties, and we used to have fun looking at all the stalls and the shops and the influx of people who came from miles away to see and be seen there. It seemed odd to us that people were so interested in Portobello. We couldn't see what all the fuss was about really.

 *Brian Collins:*

Shepherd's was our nearest shop, 50 yards from our house. It was a funny little shop. Outside it had one poster showing what was going to be on at the Odeon and one poster showing what was going to be on at the ABC, and that's how we decided which cinema to go. I should have nicked some of those posters.

Round the corner from where I lived in Penzance Place was Addison Avenue. It was a very salubrious street, where Roger Mayne lived. It was where wealthy people lived. I knew some of the people he photographed, went to school with them and played with them in places like Avondale Park. My mum had a cleaning job cleaning a very nice house in Addison Avenue for a family who were very prosperous. It always struck me, the range between the haves and the have nots just a few minutes apart. Just a few minutes from me was St James' Square, which had posh houses on the same scale as Southam Street only a mile and a half away but these houses were well preserved, whereas the houses in Southam Street where my auntie lived were neglected and run-down. In St James' Square there might be a family of four people in one house. In Southam Street there might be thirty people living in one house.

We didn't have a garden so, as children, we spent a lot of time outside in the street kicking a ball around or whatever. There were very few cars around but, if one came along, you would just move to one side to let it pass, then carry on playing. The great thing for us was the rec around the corner, Avondale Park. That attracted kids from all over. You made friends and you made enemies there, kids from Wilsham Street, Kenley Street, Princedale Road and the other side of Avondale Park, Nottingwood House and Walmer Road. Then, there were huge concrete goals at each end with sometimes fifty boys playing football. It was quite an education going there from an early age, meeting older boys that could strike fear into me, but it was a great place to grow up.

Portobello Road became a very fashionable street in the mid-Sixties. The other side of the bridge, Lord Kitchener's Valet sold ex-military jackets including red hussars' jackets. It was a place where trendy people shopped and where they drank. It was the time of swinging London and Portobello Road was up there as a destination to visit.

Susan Mcmahon:

Out the back of us was what we called the Shanty Town. It was really run-down as people started leaving. There was one basement they filled up with mattresses and I remember my brother jumping from the pavement onto the mattresses. We used to play outside all the time. That was the norm. We used to scrape between the paving stones with lolly sticks to collect the dirt to make mud pies. We would get filthy.

Down the road was a convent with blossom hanging over the walls. We would collect it and sell them for a few pennies. We would go round asking people if they wanted to buy them. I think they felt sorry for us. At the end of Tavistock Road by Westbourne Park tube, the buses used to park there sometimes and we used to sit on the buses.

Tommy the totter used to come round shouting 'Rag an' bo'. My mum would sometimes go and have a look at what he'd got. She would buy anything off him, clothes, household stuff, lamps, rugs. He would go round all the big houses round Westbourne Grove buying. I used to feed his horse. He was based round Latimer Road way.

I remember my first curry. We had an African, Joe, live down the road and he cooked us a curry. I was about 3. My dad went in the pub one day with Joe and the man behind the bar said, 'I'll serve you but I'm not serving him.' My dad said, 'What are you on about? We're together.' My dad was disgusted so he walked out. There were Irish, blacks in the street. We all got along and were in and out of each other's houses. Everyone got along. There would sometimes be shouting and screaming in the street with neighbours arguing with each other but it would all be forgotten the next day. I remember when the carnival started in 1966. There used to be a lot of floats and steel bands before the music systems came in in the Seventies when the carnival got bigger and bigger.

five

Boys and Girls Come out to Play

ᐁ Frank Hale:

It was tenpence to get in the pictures. We used to go to the old bug'ole every Saturday morning. We tried to get our friends in through the back door but the manageress, who was called Hilda, was on to it. We had a couple of queer fellas, one of them was called Barney. He used to go in the bug'ole and fall asleep and stay there all day. You could smoke in cinemas then so all the kids would go up to him and put burn holes in his mac so he would wake up and there would be about a hundred burn holes in it. When I was 13, there were some kids from out of the area in the bug'ole flicking bits of paper at us. We told them to pack it up but they wouldn't stop so I ran across the back of the seats silhouetted against the screen and punched this bloke and then they stopped.

There was a phone box on the corner of Westbourne Park Road and Kensington Park Road. We had some fun with that phone box. We would put stink bombs in there sometimes. We never let them off, just leave them on the floor so, when people went in, they would tread on them and the stink would come up. We would be watching and we would be in hysterics while they would be standing outside trying to carry on with their phone call. At the end of the street was an old Jewish woman. We hardly ever saw her except at her window upstairs. She used to have a bad chest and produced a lot of phlegm, which she collected in a bowl. If we were making a lot of noise in the street, she would throw the phlegm out the window on us. It was all over the pavement.

We were only young kids and didn't know about any prejudice but the Jewish children kept themselves to themselves and didn't want to play with us. After the war, we noticed they used to queue at the sweet shop, maybe thirty of them with their ration coupons. We found out our parents used to change their sweet coupons with their parents for butter or egg coupons and that's why we didn't have any sweets. We decided one day to have a go

Girls playing 'London to Paris', a form of hopscotch, in Portland Road, 1957. The fact that the girls are literally playing in the street, as did boys, tells its own story about the volume of traffic at that time, as well as the lack of open spaces to play in. This part of Portland Road still survives.

Adventure playgrounds, like this one in Clydesdale Road in 1959, were created after the war, mostly on bomb sites, to provide open spaces for children to play in. Boys and girls almost always played their own games in separate groups.

at them so we got a load of specky fruit from the market and belted the synagogue with it. As far as we were concerned, they were a group of people getting all the sweets.

I would play outside all the time. I would come home from school, grab a slice of bread and jam and we would go out until it got dark. When I was 10, I got my first pair of skates and we skated all the way to Perivale. There was four of us, left about half past nine in the morning and didn't get back until ten o'clock at night.

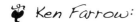 *Ken Farrow:*

I would go swimming at Wedlake Baths and, in the summer, I would go swimming in the canal. I would hop over the factory, which was between our house and the canal. We had a short ladder up to the roof on top of the press where dad kept his pigeons and then another ladder the other side down to the towpath by the canal. I would go swimming there nearly every night in the summer. It was better than the baths because there weren't the bloody little kids in the way. One day I was playing truant hiding under ha'penny steps and two boys came along and chucked me in. They lived along Bosworth Road between Hazlewood and Golborne Gardens but that didn't put me off swimming.

Margaret Burdsey (née Traies):

We would go to Lancaster Road Baths sometimes. It was only tuppence to swim in the small pool or fourpence in the big pool. There were slipper baths in there as well so people could go and have a bath. It was cubicles with duck boards on the floor and cockroaches running underneath, and you all got verrucas as a result of running around barefoot. There were curtains across the cubicles and sometimes the curtain would come unhooked. In Lancaster Road Baths, you could get a penny slice of bread with a thin coating of jam on it, no butter. When we came out, we would sometimes get half a roll and dripping for a ha'penny or we would go across the road and get black bubblegum and lemonade powder and we would chew it all up together just for something to do. Our dad used to say bubblegum was made out of boiled down horses' hooves and, if you swallowed it, it would get wound round your insides but it didn't put us off.

Maureen Rafferty (née Coker):

I've known Patsy Shepherd since primary school. I used to stop at her house on Saturday nights when my mum and dad went to the Warwick for a few drinks. We used to watch them at the window coming back from the pub singing away. I would go to Harrow Road police station sometimes and make out I'd got lost and they would give me a cup of tea and a biscuit or a slice of cake. I think a lot of us did that. Before bonfire night, I would go round to the Prince of Wales in Harrow Road all dressed up and my face all painted up to do penny for the guy outside the cinema.

Derek Ford:

We would play marbles in the gutter because there weren't many people had cars in those days. We used to play on the bomb sites in St Charles' Square and Telford Road. There's hardly a day goes by I don't think about W10. I loved every minute of it. I can see myself playing on the bomb sites even now. There was glass, there was metal, there were holes, there were cellars, we cut our knees, played bows and arrows and Cowboys and Indians. We would go on the buses collecting tickets. We used to collect cigarette packets because they sometimes had cards inside, birds or cricketers. I remember they were in Turf cigarettes. I'd pick up the packets in the street to see if they'd left the card inside.

Alan Warner:

In Beethoven Street, we kids would play out, unlike today's kids who play in. There was a bigger family than mine who lived opposite Kerr's laundry in Herries Street, called Sampson. Tommy Sampson was my age and we went to Beethoven Street School. We were good mates. We used to play run-outs, a game where you had a base and the object of the game was to get back to base without being caught. Half of us would run off and the others had to stop you getting back.

Roger Loveridge would as often as not be with us. Rog used to knock around with us and my brother Sherby. Aunt Iris said he was like a sherbet dab when he was born and Sherby became his name from that day on. Roger was epileptic. If we were quick, we could get him out of the trance that led to a fit. I asked him what happened when he had a fit and he told me that he saw a little black speck in his peripheral vision and he couldn't stop himself from following it with his eyes and then 'bang', he was fitting. He would go into a trance but, if we grabbed him and shouted his name, sometimes he would come to. Smashing family; his dad was one of my dad's drinking pals.

❧ Richard Rowlands:

We used to make our own fun. We would make go-karts and go here and there. We would take them on to the top of Ladbroke Grove hill and come down and sometimes we would smash them to pieces. All we had was plimsolls and wellingtons and that's all anyone had. We was all in the same boat. There was a bomb site where the church was in Golborne Gardens and we used to play cricket on the pavement next to it.

We used to swim in the canal by the gasworks and we thought it was alright because it was warm there. There was all dead rats but we done it. I was over the canal with my friend one day. All we were doing was playing. We were about 13 and this copper came over and said to me 'What's your name?' and I said 'Richard Johnson' because I always used to call myself Johnson. Then he said to my friend 'What's your name?' and he said 'Archibald McGillicuddy' and the policeman hit him straight round the face and said 'Don't take the piss out of me' and it was his real name.

When we was kids we used to jump on the barges. We would go over Kensal Road and there's a narrow spot where you could jump on but the first place you could get off was Southall then we'd walk back. The men on the barges didn't care. They were pulling them along with horses. It was something to do. We used to play in the cemetery. We'd go over there of a night and frighten ourselves to death. There was youth clubs around then. We would go in the Seven Feathers, the First Feathers. There was one down the Peabody's. Connie and Bill were the people who run the one in Edenham Street.

❧ Gwen Nelson (née Martin):

When we first moved to Golborne Road I quickly made friends with a girl who lived next door to me. Yiannoula Christou was Greek Cypriot and her parents were cousins to the barbers in Kensal Road. We were always in and out of each other's homes when we weren't playing hopscotch, swinging round the lamp posts on ropes or playing up the little rec. Because there was so little traffic, children mostly played in the street. Most homes didn't have enough room for lots of energetic children to be tearing around so weekends and after school would be spent outside in all but the worst weather.

It was an unwritten rule that boys and girls played separately. In part I think this was due to the fact that most of the local schools still ran on Victorian lines with boys and girls having separate entrances and playgrounds but also no boy wanted to be seen as a sissy and their games were often rough and violent. We girls were frequently warned, 'You keep away from those boys,' even if the boys in question were, as often happened, the girls' brothers.

'Cowboys and Indians' was a favourite. Cowboys had cap guns and Indians had home made bows that fired twigs or bits of dowelling with sharpened points. Some boys also had home made carts, usually a bit of planking attached to a set of pram or bike wheels. These would be pushed along the middle of the road by one boy, the other steering the wheels with a piece of string attached to the axle. When sufficient speed had built up the pusher would jump on the back and they'd travel until friction and weight dragged it to a standstill. There was a skill in being a pusher. Too fast and you ran the risk of being left behind, if your balance wasn't right when you leapt onto the cart you'd either fall off or your weight would cause the cart to upend tumbling out both you and the driver.

'Allies' or marbles was a popular game with many rules and a language of its own. Most of the marbles were multi-coloured glass but some were also aggies, made of agate or made of alabaster. A dobber was a big marble used to hit the smaller ones. There were also large, frosted glass ones called 'bottle washers'. They came from the necks of fizzy drink bottles. The glass sphere was used to seal the top of the bottle. To call 'quitsies' meant you could stop the game without losing your marbles. 'Keepsies' meant you kept all the marbles you had won. To start a game one had to 'knuckle down', which meant to position your hand with your knuckle against the ground before firing the marble into the ring. It was taken every bit as seriously as the game of 'knock down' or flicking trading cards set up against a wall. Cigarette manufacturers would include collectible cards on a variety of themes in the packets. Cricketers, footballers, war heroes were all represented. There were more of some than others and fierce bartering took place for the rarer ones.

Girls' games were more decorous, although both sexes played 'tag'. We played games with two balls up against the wall. 'One, two three O'Leary' to which we'd add, 'I saw Bridget Geary, sitting on her bumbaleery, eating squashed tomatoes'. I think the accepted version continued 'four, five six O'Leary' up to 'ten O'Leary overball' when you'd have to swap hands catching the balls. Skipping ropes were another great favourite. It had a language of its own, crisscross, side swing, scissors were all different manoeuvres with the rope. It could be played either on one's own or with two girls swinging the rope and others jumping. If there were two swingers, two ropes could be used turning in opposite directions.

Hopscotch was played on courts marked out with chalk on the pavement. The most basic court was just numbered from one to nine with 'home' at the end where you could turn to complete the return trip. Others were more complex with double squares. Other games we played were 'oranges and lemons', 'Simon says' and 'statues'. Another popular, but less acceptable game, was to knock on someone's door and run away before they answered it. The dare was to see how long you could stand in front of the door before scarpering. If you got caught you'd likely be chased and given a good hard slap or hear the threat, 'I'll tell your mother'.

Chalk was for drawing on the pavement. Elaborate pictures were made on the stone slabs only to be washed off in the next shower of rain or smeared by the boots of passers-by. We were allowed to draw on the pavement with impunity nor were we told off for another favourite pastime, swinging on the lamp post. Lamp posts had projections jutting out either side just below the light. I think these were to support a ladder if any work needed to be done on the light. We had a long piece of sash cord which was knotted to form a loop and then throw over the projection.

The bomb site on Golborne Gardens was a favourite playground as parts of walls were still standing and the delineation of rooms still visible. Yiannoula and I would play 'house' and set up chairs and tables from bricks and bits of wood. Sometimes we'd come across bits of broken china and other things to decorate 'our homes'. In summer the bomb site was a wonderful garden. As well as daisies and dandelions, which we called 'piss the beds', a tall pink flower called Rosebay Willow Herb also grew.

A favourite place was the little rec. I would pass through it on my way to and from St Mary's School, lingering longer on the way home and playing on the seesaw, swings and witch's hat. One of the children's favourite tricks was to hang upside down on the witch's hat while keeping out a weather eye for the park keeper. The playground area was all tarmac but there were very few accidents. I can only remember one girl falling off the witch's hat and breaking her arm although a few managed to go over the head of the rocking horse when it was cranked up to maximum pitch. Further afield was the Little Wormwood Scrubs off Delgarno Gardens, a bit of a hike to get there but it was an enjoyable walk down Barlby Road past St Charles' Hospital.

Saturday mornings was pocket money time. A shilling to go to the Saturday morning Minors at the Prince of Wales cinema in Harrow Road. Sixpence entry and sixpence for sweets. The session started with the ABC Minors song. I can't recall all the words but it ended 'We're the children of the ABC' shouted at the top of our lungs. Usually a children's newsreel was followed by several cartoons, Tom and Jerry, Mickey Mouse, Bugs Bunny, Popeye and then the serial with its cliffhanger ending. As well as the pictures, children's birthdays would be announced and the birthday boy or girl would go up on stage to receive a small gift. Once a year there would be a fancy dress competition with a prize for the best boy and girl. One year, Dad hired costumes for the Bisto Kids for myself and Yiannoula but, come the Friday afternoon, they hadn't arrived. Panic set in and poor mum sat up half the night sewing me a belly dancer's outfit from old curtains and a velvet bolero of hers while Yannoula had to make do with my First Communion dress and veil and pretend she was a bride.

Charlie Phillips:

I made friends. I think people took sympathy on me. On the way to school, we would sometimes get involved in punch-ups or we used to play on the bomb sites with the white kids I made friends with.

Margaret Stedman (née Riddick):

Half the things we did then they wouldn't be allowed to do today like go on a bomb site. We played on the bomb site in Hazlewood Crescent. We would say 'We're playing on the debris'. Firework night was always there on the bomb site in Hazlewood Crescent. I wasn't allowed fireworks so I went to look at the fireworks with my dad. I wasn't allowed to go on my own. People would have bonfires they'd actually built in the middle of the road.

Ray Matthews:

I remember playing football in the street and the girls playing hopscotch, skipping or two balls up the wall. We played marbles in the gutter or flicks where you placed cards against the wall and, if you flicked a card and knocked them over you won the card. There was also penny nearest the wall. If we didn't have chalk to mark a wicket on the wall, we looked for a white dog turd and used it as chalk. It always fell apart.

🌻 Babs Coker:

Most of my time was spent in the local parks, Barlby Road rec and St Marks Park where they had a paddling pool and also a stage where you could watch shows. I remember watching Pinocchio the puppet there once. We used to play games like run outs, hopscotch, five bucks and knock down ginger. Over the Scrubs, we used to play in the war bunkers, that's if the park keeper never caught us. They went underground and we had great fun in them. Also down Barlby Road, there was a mews where we used to go because there was train carriages to play in.

I used to dress my brother Gerald up as a guy before bonfire night, sit him on Ladbroke Grove bridge and tell him not to move so we could collect some money for fireworks. I went scrumpying and got chased by the lady whose trees we were taking apples from. I also went blackberry picking. We were out nearly all day. I used to go swimming in Wedlake Baths then got a bag of chips with crackling on the way home.

🌻 Alan Peverall:

I used to play the usual games like football, cricket, marbles and conkers, and we made go-karts out of planks of wood and pram wheels and raced them around the streets. We used play in parks like the little rec, St Mark's and Little Scrubs, and play on the swings. The jerker was my favourite. We also used to go over to the big Scrubs where there were the remains of gun emplacements from the war. We used to explore the tunnels. I had a friend called Stephen Choules who I used to go to the park and play football with. We were sitting in the garden in the little rec one day when we heard a big bang. We looked through the railings set in the garden wall and saw a car crashed opposite St Mary's School and people running around. We didn't go into the street but it turned out that it was a robbery taking place.

When they pulled the houses down in Bosworth Road opposite the Roman Catholic church, the cellars were still there so we made a camp in one. We raided Askey's wafer factory in Kensal Road and took the boxes back to camp and used them for supplies. It was fun but, thinking back on it, it was pretty dangerous messing about in a derelict cellar but, in them days, you didn't care. Most kids were doing similar things or worse.

🕯 Reg Thackeray:

Outside our house in St Ervans, we had a lamp post with horns. People now don't believe the street lamps used to have them. We used to put a rope round one of the horns and swing round and round. We played cricket up against a pillar box as the wicket. If you whacked the ball down the airy, you were out and if you smashed someone's window you scattered. It cost 10s to replace a window. I remember we had to pay for one once.

🫖 Roger Rogowski:

Back then, boys did a lot of collecting and collecting coins was quite popular. This was helped because, even in the Sixties, there were still halfpennies and pennies in circulation dating back to the 1860s, so there was history to be found in our change. A lot of the coins were almost worn flat but it meant that boys could start their own collection for not very much. Collecting and swapping cards was also popular. Thanks to my mum being an Olympic-level tea drinker, I collected Brooke Bond Tea cards, which always featured educational subjects like 'Wild Flowers of Britain' and 'Wildlife in Danger'. They were free as my mum bought the tea but worth paying for was a series of trading cards in packets of bubblegum featuring the American Civil War. These were swapped enthusiastically by a lot of the boys in my class and featured gory scenes of soldiers being bayonetted, crushed, blown up, burned or, maybe if they were lucky, only shot.

Another draw on my money later was football as some of us boys would sometimes get together in the school playground on Friday and decide to go to a match the next day. We would either meet at the No. 28 bus stop opposite Westbourne Park station and take the bus to Stamford Bridge or meet at the station to take the train to Shepherd's Bush for Loftus Road.

Standing on the terraces at Stamford Bridge cost two and six for boys and a programme was sixpence, the same cost as the bus fare, so football on Saturday was easily affordable from my pocket money and something we could decide to do almost on the spur of the moment, usually about once a month. It was about the same price to get into Loftus Road to watch Third Division football, so Chelsea was usually our first choice. As the turnstiles at Stamford Bridge stood on Fulham Road at that time, fans could move about freely once inside behind the stands and opposing sets of fans would often pass each other to change ends at half time, either behind the main stand or the west terrace, without any trouble. As small boys, we always stood down the front of the terraces close to the pitch. At the time there was a greyhound track round the track, which was illuminated by lights, which were folded flat when football was on. The trouble was, when the action was close to our end, we couldn't see what the players were doing below their knees or where the ball was. One time, we set out at our usual time to watch Chelsea play Manchester United and the crowd at the turnstiles was immense. Adults were pressing in on our small gang from all sides, the crowd was barely moving and we could hardly breathe as people pushed forward. As much as we wanted to see the match, we were in fear of injury more and decided to struggle against the crowd to get out.

I always had a few fireworks to let off with Con in the Cullen's backyard on bonfire night and, when we were younger, our mums would take us to see the big bonfire and the older children letting off their fireworks on the bomb site in Golborne Road, where Hazlewood Tower now stands, until we were old enough to join them on our own. Bonfire night was always eagerly anticipated for weeks before. Assorted scrap timber and unwanted or broken furniture was piled up in a heap on the bomb site, fireworks were sold loose or in boxes and appeared in the shops and children would set up a pitch with their home-made guys, usually close to a pub or shops to collect penny for the guy. Penny bangers and jumping jacks were always fun to let off near groups of unsuspecting adults and bonfire night itself was always full of explosions, noise, smoke and the smell of gunpowder.

My pocket money was supplemented by being in the church choir at St Helen's just off St Quintin Avenue. I got 6d for attending Friday evening choir practice and for each Sunday service, and 2s 6d for a wedding. It was an impressive choir comprising male and female choristers as wells as boys. The music didn't always go well. Before one wedding, our organist said she wasn't able to play that Saturday but that she'd arranged for her nephew to play instead. He must have been very nervous because it sounded more like Les Dawson playing with wrong notes all over the place. As young as I was, I felt for the bride and groom on their special day and I hope they were able to laugh it off afterwards.

Bob Crawley, one of my classmates at St Andrew's, persuaded me to join the choir and we would walk between our homes in Kensal Road and Bosworth Road for Friday night choir practice and services at the church without any problem. One dark night, we both had a narrow escape when walking to choir practice. We were on the zebra crossing on Ladbroke Grove at the top of Chesterton Road when a speeding car came out of nowhere and caught me a glancing blow and sped off without even braking. Other than a badly cut leg, I was OK but, if I had taken just one more step forward, it would have been much more serious. A while later, I joined a Boy Scout troop, which met somewhere in Paddington. We wore traditional khaki uniforms with shorts and campaign-style hats. We probably looked like extras from *It Ain't Half Hot Mum*, although that was on TV much later. The troop met on Friday evenings at the same time as choir practice but learning handicrafts and playing boisterous games was a lot more fun than singing hymns, so I took a pay cut and put an end to my singing career.

Because we were fairly close to the BBC television studios, the local roads were sometimes used to shoot on location. At least one episode of *Z Cars* was filmed in the area, in Appleford Road. I remember peering into one of those fabulous white Ford Zephyrs to see actors James Ellis and I think Colin Welland sitting in the front seats looking a bit terrified to be surrounded by dozens of small boys. Hazlewood Crescent was used as the location for a play shown on ITV in 1964. Called *The Crunch* and written by Nigel Kneale, it featured a fictional country's embassy in which someone had planted a nuclear warhead threatening to destroy London, which was being evacuated. Most of the houses in the area were impressive architecturally and Hazlewood Crescent must have contained houses that were less dilapidated than most so one of them could pass for an embassy in one of the more upmarket parts of London. The street was full of arc lights, trailing cables, impressive cameras and vans full of equipment, and crowds of curious children.

The side streets between the canal and the railway line, where there was less traffic than on Kensal and Golborne Roads, were usually more or less full of children. Edenham Street was usually my destination as it was closest. Whenever I walk round the local side streets that still exist, like Hazlewood

Crescent, Golborne Gardens and Adair Road now, I can't get used to how quiet they are. About a year before we moved, in 1965, the Bird family moved in next door having recently arrived from Calcutta. Dad Kevin and mum Doreen and their three children Kevin, Michael and Jacky, all impressed me by how well they and their children spoke and how well-behaved they were, in contrast to most of the boys and girls I usually hung around with. It was Jacky with her long dark hair and who was 14 and two years than me, who made the biggest impression. She would often come round to our house and we would sometimes sit and talk and giggle on the sofa in an only semi-innocent way.

Mossy Condon:

Edenham Street or Southam Street, there were always children playing, skipping or playing hopscotch. We would throw our coats down in Hazlewood Crescent to make a goal, there was only two cars in our road. The priest had one and the postman. You would never see a car go through there. The priest's car might move on a Saturday and that was it and he would be parked in the same place all week. You would put your coats down and play football for two or three hours and you wouldn't see anybody.

When the houses started to empty out when Hazlewood and Adair Towers were built, people moved out of the houses into the towers, so the houses became derelict and we used to play in the empty houses. Going round you'd often find things like a big rocking horse, people would leave in there. You could play in there and make your own fun. Micky Daley was my best friend. He lived opposite above the library in Golborne Road and we got two tin cans and a very long piece of string and we run a line down. We run the string over the top of the telephone wires from my fourth-floor balcony down to his balcony on the second floor. It worked quite well until someone cut the string.

Barbara Reynolds (née Murray):

I never really moved out of the street. We used to swing round the lamp post on a bit of rope, play rounders in the street, run outs, football, cricket. We used to play a lot of hopscotch, London to Paris, and skipping. In the school holidays, the cinema van used to come round so we could watch the pictures and I used to go to the play centre at Bevington School. They used to stay open during the school holidays so children who had free meals could go there to play. I used to go to the Saturday morning pictures at the Prince of Wales. Sometimes they would call us up on stage for things like yo-yo competitions and show films like *Old Mother Riley*.

When they were knocking down the houses in Southam Street, we got a length of rope and got into one of the houses, went through the front door, up the stairs, opened the window and we tied the rope to the top and slid down the outside on the rope. I was crapping myself but, if everyone else is doing it, you have to do it.

Bob Crawley:

When I was at Thomas Jones School, someone came in one day to ask if anyone wanted to join the choir at St Helen's Church. They paid two and six for a wedding and one and six a week for the choir practice and two Sunday services. If you got three weddings on the trot, you were quids in, so I joined up. As a choir boy at St Helen's Church I remember seeing the cast of *Softly, Softly*, including Stratford Johns, and *Z Cars* using the church hall for rehearsals. *Steptoe and Son* was made in the area and one of the scenes in the film version was made in our flat in Trellick Tower when we moved there.

As children, we had the run of demolition and building sites to play on, so long as Mum and Dad didn't find out. We would jump over the fence and go around with those long weights from the sash windows in empty houses and smash holes in the walls. Watching the big ball demolish houses or seeing the workman drag a steel hawser on a tractor through a row of houses was great fun. On occasion the demolition work would disturb hordes of rats that would then run down the road. Some of the more confident kids would try and hit them with bricks as they ran past. One day I injured myself and had to go home and lie about how it happened or they would have beaten the life out of me if I'd told them how I'd done it. It was like an adventure going round to see what they'd left behind. There was nothing of any value. I found a shove ha'penny board. You could look in the old cupboards and find things like old irons. If we were playing football in the street next to the demolition site and knocked the ball over the fence, one of us would distract the guard dogs at the other end while someone would climb over and get the ball back.

We had go-karts with pram wheels on that we would push around and second-hand bikes from Portobello Road in the market, a pound or thirty bob each. If you had your bike nicked, you could go down there and sometimes see your own bike and buy it back. A bike gave you freedom to travel further, like down to the Little Scrubs where there was a short cinder track we used to race our bikes round. We would also go to the little rec to play. Other games included hopscotch, run outs, both on our feet or, for more excitement, on bikes, buck and four stones. Skating with the old-fashioned wheeled skates was popular, although my friend Graham Wheeler caused problems by using skates with steel wheels rather than rubber-coated ones, and made an absolute racket. Football in the car park at the back of Bosworth House was always popular. The space was supposedly for parking but few people owned cars and it was never used for that purpose. The only downside of the football was that the goal at one end was a garage door directly below flat No. 3 and it wasn't that infrequent that the ball was shot too high and went straight through No. 3's kitchen window.

Swimming was also a popular pastime and we would normally use Wedlake Baths – large pool in the summer, small pool in the winter – but for a change we would use Lancaster Road Baths. That had the benefit of a small room serving drinks and cakes, and they always had my favourite cake, bread pudding. For a laugh, at Wedlake, we would climb up to the balcony and jump into the deep end. I don't think the attendant was that bothered. The pool had a rail round it where you used to hold on when first learning to swim. The changing rooms were boys on one side and girls on the other side. In the summer we ventured further afield to the Serpentine Lido.

I was in the Scouts in the 66th Kensington, which met in a hall in Kensal Road. The bloke who ran it ended up living with the Akela, who came over from New Zealand for a few months. They ended up getting married and moving to New Zealand, and the troop folded up. It was a big troop at the time. There were four patrols with about ten or twelve Scouts in each one. We did games and rough and tumble things, learned how to make fires, how to do orienteering, put a tent up, how to keep milk fresh in the summer by digging holes, how to filter canal water with charcoal and blotting paper so you could drink it after boiling it. I paid a shilling a week to go along. It was a great experience.

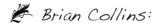 *Brian Collins:*

From a very early age, going to the cinema on a Saturday morning was a big part of my life. There were so many cinemas to choose from, like the ABC and the Odeon in Westbourne Grove. The one we liked best was the Odeon in Kensington High Street because it was the smartest, which involved a bit of a walk through Holland Park. We tended to avoid the bug'ole in Portobello Road. Our house was the nearest to the cinema so there would be about twelve to eighteen boys arrive at our house to pick up my brother and me and then we would make our way through the park and go to the Odeon. One thing that stuck in my mind was the old Commonwealth Institute being constructed. We saw it going up as we walked past with that extraordinary roof.

For six old pence, it was amazing entertainment going there. Saturday morning pictures would start about nine in the morning and finish about twelve. There might be some sort of Western or some sort of spy film. I remember one called *Operation Third Form*, which was a film about young schoolboys being spies. They would have these cliffhangers, so you would have to go next week to see what happens. In the interlude they would get audience participation. One day they said, 'You might have heard about a new dance sensation called the twist and we need ten children up here on stage to take part.' A friend of mine, Peter, who was up for anything, went up there and we all cheered for Peter. If we had any money left, we would sometimes take a detour on the way back and sit in a little caff in Norland Gardens, I think it was called The Silver Badge, near Winkler's where we got our jeans when we were a bit older. You could have a big mug of tea and a ham roll and, paying sixpence for the cinema, you would still have change out of two bob after going to the caff, so money went a long way. My mum would give me two bob pocket money from her purse every Saturday morning until I got my first job when I was 12, then the pocket money stopped.

When I was 9 or 10, I would get a Red Rover with some of my friends and jump on a bus and we would go everywhere. One day with my mate Steve, we walked to Kensington High Street and saw this bus for London Airport so we jumped on it and went out to the airport. We went into the terminal building and saw all the destinations like San Francisco and Cape Town and it all seemed so exotic and exciting to a boy from Notting Dale. These people seemed so rich and I just had a day out at Littlehampton.

Susan Mcmahon:

We went to Wedlake Baths. We spent all day and at the end my hair would be bleached with the chlorine. Men's changing rooms was on one side, ladies' the other side with the shower at one end and the pool in the middle. I think the shower was constantly on and we would go under there when we got cold. I tried getting out of the pool one day and my hand slipped and I bashed my chin on the edge of the pool and had to have stitches. They had baths in there. People would go on Friday or Saturday night and have a bath, older people from 18 upwards, and you could do your washing there. On the way home we would get a portion of chips.

six

Schooldays

‿ *Frank Hale:*

I went to St Francis' Primary School in Treadgold Street. The headmistress was Mrs King. There were some characters went to that school. One boy who went there for a while was a bully. He used to take our dinner money off us standing there with his henchmen. You had to hand your money over otherwise you'd get beat up, so we had to go without food. Although it was rough, there was a code. Fighting was with fists one on one with everyone else standing round watching until we got fed up with fighting each other. No one used knives or ganged up on someone except the bullies taking our dinner money. I used to walk there on my own. In those days, people didn't really move out of their area, so everyone knew everyone else. Then I went to St Michael's School in Artesian Road. It was next to St Mary of the Angels on the corner of Moorhouse Road. It was a very small school. The headmaster was Jock McGibbon, who seemed to like caning you. I was only there a year before we moved.

🐦 *Ken Farrow:*

I started at St Andrew's in 1949, then I went to St Mary's in 1952 and stayed until summer 1955. I remember, when I was at St Andrew's, we were helped up onto the wall between the playground and the railway to watch the train taking King George VI's body from Paddington to Windsor after his funeral in 1952 and again when Queen Mary died in 1953. I used to help Mr Lovell, the caretaker at St Andrew's, by bringing the milk in and delivering them to the classrooms, then I went to Cardinal Manning. I had to make sure my sisters got to school and I was always late to school because of them so I used to get one or two of the best. I had two elder sisters who could easily have taken them but they didn't.

🍬 Margaret Burdsey (née Traies):

As you went into Wornington Road School, there was a sweet shop next door called The Cabin. I never bought anything in The Cabin because we lived in a sweet shop but that was where the children would come out of school and spend their money and they could buy a small glass of Tizer for a penny.

I remember that first day at Wornington Road Infants. There was a toy on every chair. They used to get these canvas camp beds out in the afternoon for the nursery class so we could have a sleep. Wornington Road Infants was on the ground floor and the secondary school was on the floor above. It was so lovely. The head teacher had trained at the Froebel Institute and it was quite

Derek Ford (second left, top row) at Oxford Gardens Primary School, 1955. The school still operates today in its original building.

The first-year class at St Andrew's School in Emslie Horniman Pleasance, May Day 1959. This little park in Middle Row was always called 'the little rec'. Roger Rogowski is third boy from the left; Krys Mozdzynski, third boy from the right; and Barbara Reynolds (*née* Murray) is fourth right in the front row. The ornamental garden has now been beautifully restored.

a forward-thinking school. All the doors opened onto the playground. We loved it. She was very into music and drama and every Friday afternoon, one class or another would do a play for the rest of the school. We used to have visual aids for reading, big pictures round the room that the teacher drew with a sentence underneath and the story I remember most of all was 'My Little Black Sambo'. There were very few Afro-Caribbean people in the area at that time. When we were in the top class, we were allowed to go down and wake the infants up and read to them.

Jane and I then went to Barlby Road Juniors. That was a big old red brick building that's now demolished and is now a single-storey building. In my class at Barlby, only three children passed their eleven-plus and only two of those went to grammar schools because the mum and dad of the third one decided they couldn't afford the uniform so they didn't go, and that wasn't an unusual story. The girls went to Holland Park or Fulham County. On the other side of the girls' playground at Barlby Road was what we called the shed where you could go if it was raining. At the back of the shed was an old home economics room, which dated back to those days when the girls learned about cookery. There was an art room across the boys' playground where we used to wash our inkwells on a Friday afternoon. We had an open fire in our classroom.

✿ Jane Traies:

I'm sorry to say I bought something in The Cabin. Our mum and dad tried so hard to better themselves and wanted to be respectable and one of their ways of being respectable was we weren't allowed to have bubblegum, so the one thing I would always buy on the way to school in The Cabin was bubblegum and I got found out because I collected the photos of film stars that were inside the packets. One day my mum said, 'Where did you get all those cards?'

Wornington Road Infants was ahead of its time. You would go in in the morning, choose which table you sat at and you had an hour of free activity. You painted, you drew, you played and then you did your lessons and then every Friday every class did a play in the hall. We read with a reading scheme called Mac and Tosh and then we went into Janet and John. We were scruffy little people. We were the most disadvantaged children but that was such a good start in life. They used to hand out cod liver oil capsules at school and a lot of boys used to put them in the inkwell to avoid swallowing them.

After Wornington Road Infants, I went to Barlby Road Juniors. In the years after the war, there was great poverty so, at Barlby Road, there were things like a boot club where children brought in a penny each week to fill stamps up in a card and, when they had filled the card, they got a grant to buy a pair of shoes. We were on the receiving end of a great deal of charity. There was also something called the Flower Lovers' League, which gave a daffodil bulb to every child in the autumn and three nasturtium seeds to every child in the spring. You would have a set date when you had to come back to the school with your lovely pot with your daffodil in it and you would get a certificate. Everyone got a certificate with a photo of a daffodil on it, not what yours looked like at all. It said, 'Thank you flower lover for growing this plant.' In the autumn you brought in your pot of nasturtiums and you got another certificate. People who lived in dark places like basements, their daffodil would be about a foot long with no flower on but they still brought them in.

🦋 John Traies:

We used to have a sleep in the afternoons at Wornington Road Infants and the girl that used to sleep next to me in class used to wet herself every day.

🌿 Pauline Clark (née Harding):

My school was just down the end of the road. It was St Andrew's and it was called the doll's house as it was so small. I only went in five classes and was in the top class for two years. We only had a fireplace in one corner of the classroom, so it was cold at the back of the class.

〜 Maureen Rafferty (née Coker):

I went to Florence Gladstone School in Wornington Road then they changed it to a boys' school in 1959 and I had to go to Ladbroke Girls' School in Lancaster Road opposite St Mark's Park.

🦐 Derek Ford:

The first thing I ever remember was all the birthday cards on the mantelpiece. I remember my first day at Oxford Gardens School vividly. My mum took me holding my hand. She took me in the classroom and the next thing I remember I looked out the window and Mum was waving and off she went and I think I cried all day. I couldn't believe I'd been left. After a couple of days I thought this is what it's going to be, sitting in the same seat listening to Mrs Hedges, my first teacher, so I accepted it.

At the age of 8, I went to the junior school at Oxford Gardens. They made you eat your dinner. I hated greens and I hated semolina and rice with a bit of jam in the middle. About half ten or eleven, you would get the smell of the dinners cooking and I would cringe. I was always the last one to finish. The dinner ladies would stand there until I finished but I was getting a decent meal. I wasn't the best of pupils but I loved sports. I swam for Kensington and so did my brother and got certificates and medals I wish I'd kept. My brother got even more. He was the champion of Kensington. He smoked since the age of about 10 or 11. I remember my dad turning his pockets out looking for cigarettes.

 *Gwen Nelson (née Martin):*

When we lived in Stockwell, Mum used to hand-make my dresses with ruching, frills and smocking, and my hair would be coaxed each night into ringlets with strips of rag. I attended tap dancing and ballet classes and was useless at both due to a chronic lack of rhythm. When we moved to Golborne Road, I was so teased at Wornington Road School because I looked and sounded different from the rag-tag children who attended that Mum had my hair cut into a straight bob and ran me up some plain gingham dresses that washed into shapelessness. My accent was still South London but at least I didn't look obviously different.

I only stayed less than a year at Wornington Road. As well as the bullying, the level of teaching left much to be desired. Mum told me I went, at 6 years old knowing my six, seven and eight times tables and left having forgotten my three times table, so I was enrolled at St Mary's Catholic School on East Row. St Mary's was a very different experience. It was a much smaller school and exercised a far more autocratic regime. Sister Mary Austin was a much feared and respected headmistress. Small and bustling in her black habit and white wimple, she had the uncanny ability to suddenly appear just as you were thinking of misbehaving. We suspected it was divine intervention as we were told that God was always watching us.

In my first year Sister Mary Monica was our class teacher. Young, quietly spoken and gentle in her ways, she punished rarely, preferring instead to explain that our behaviour was hurting Jesus, who had died for our sins. The worst punishment I can recall receiving from her was being made to stand in the corner after I was caught talking in class. Unfortunately her reluctance to physically punish and instead appeal to our fear of offending Jesus had the effect of giving me a severe guilt complex. I was very happy at St Mary's and my end of year report for 1954 stated, 'Gwendolen is a bright, intelligent child and has made marvellous progress in her work, though her writing could be much better.' St Mary's was the first school where I had to wear a uniform. It was a grey pleated skirt, deep golden blouse and vermilion cardigan. I was one of the few children whose parents could afford full uniform and as a consequence I was always placed in the front row when we had school concerts. Regrettably, a complete uniform was not matched with any musical ability. Teachers had long accepted my lack of musical ear and instructed me to just mouth the words and not actually sing.

My second year at St Mary's was under the auspices of Miss Kenny. She had a reputation of being extremely strict and standing no nonsense from any of her pupils. Fortunately she seemed to take a liking to me and I don't recall any punishments. When I was at St Mary's there was a graded system of payment for school meals depending on how many children in a family were at the school. I think it was 1s per week if there was only one child, 10d for a second child and 8d per child thereafter. Meals were basic: meat stew, macaroni cheese, sausages and always, on Friday, fish, all accompanied with over-boiled greens and lots of spud. There was always a bulky dessert: treacle pudding, apple sponge, rice pudding, semolina or snot and bogey, as we called tapioca. The food was cooked at a central kitchen and delivered by van in the late morning. You were stood over by the teacher on dining room duty to make sure you cleaned your plate. Many of the children relied on school dinner as the only real food they had and it was easy enough to pass something I disliked to someone who wasn't quite so fussy when the teacher's back was turned.

Milk arrived early in the morning and it was the task of milk monitors to carry in the crates and stack them by the surround of the large open fire in the corner of the classroom until morning break. In summer the bottles remained cool but in winter, with the fire stacked high and throwing out fierce heat just a short distance away, they were often thickened and malodorous come mid-morning. Since infancy I had been unable to drink raw milk, vomiting if I was given any. Because the free milk scheme was compulsory, Mum had to write a note every term asking for me to be excused. Either she forgot to write it or I would forget to take it with me, so the first couple of days of term, I had to endure being forced to drink milk, gagging as I did so and then the embarrassment of heaving it up only minutes later. I recall one time facing Miss Kenny as my gut revolted and having the satisfaction of coating her Donegal tweed skirt with a white, mucous deposit. As well as school milk we also received a daily teaspoon of malt and a tablespoon full of concentrated orange juice. Malt was dispensed from a large tin. One spoon did for all of us. Some children loved its taste and would try and get a second helping. There was also a healthy black market for the spoonful you hadn't swallowed. It'd be hawked out and given to someone else who did like it like a bird feeding its young but, if you were caught, smacks all round.

Our health was taken very seriously. There were regular visits from the school dental nurse to extract milk teeth or make small fillings. She had a portable drill that required a foot-operated turntable to make the drill revolve, consequently its rhythm varied depending on her level of concentration. She didn't use any analgesia and her visits were dreaded. The other regular visitor was the school health nurse, also known as Nitty Nora as one of her tasks was to search children's heads for parasites. She had a steel comb, nicknamed the nit rake, and a jar of disinfectant. The comb would be plunged into the jar, then drawn through your hair, scraping the scalp often to the point of drawing blood. If you were uncontaminated you stood on one side of the class but if you had an infestation you stood on the other, your name was taken and a letter written to your parents proclaiming you were unclean and ordering treatment. Kerosene was a standard treatment to kill head lice and their eggs and for days after Nitty Nora's visit the school stunk of it.

It was at St Mary's that I met the girl who was to become my best friend. Maureen and I were both voracious readers and seen by the teachers as being 'gifted'. End of year exams brought out our competitive spirit and curiosity as to who would come first in class. Invariably it was Maureen who pipped me at the post. Overall my subject marks were slightly higher but her handwriting was much neater and her marks for that much higher than mine, which clinched her place at the top of the class. Other friends were Ann, who sat next to me in class and fascinated me as she always had one hand up her knickers during lessons; the Maloney girls, who lived in Hazlewood Crescent; and Sheila Ryan, who lived in Edenham Street.

There was a groundsman at the school who was responsible for sweeping the playgrounds, cleaning the classrooms and general maintenance. He was a shadowy figure who always wore a brown cotton coat. One weekend I decided to go up to the school because I'd left something behind when school finished. I climbed over the fence and was making my way to the classroom when I was suddenly set upon by the groundsman's fox terrier. He didn't bite me but was yapping and nipping at my ankles. I had always been timid around dogs and panicking, started screaming, which excited the terrier even more. Fortunately, the groundsman was close by and called off his dog but it took me years before I felt comfortable again when a dog was nearby.

Once a week our class was taken to Wedlake Baths for swimming lessons. It was a dark Victorian building that was both a bathhouse and a swimming pool. The swimming pool reeked of chlorine and was surrounded by small cubicles where one changed. The doors of the cubicles could only be locked from the inside and theft from them was quite common unless you kept a close watch. The pool was divided into the deep end and the shallow end. The latter was about 3ft and the other end about 6ft. We beginners entered the shallow end and spread ourselves out along the wall of the pool, grasping the rail that ran around the pool, interrupted only by steps leading into it. First lessons were to hold onto the rail and kick out our legs behind us so we were floating. Once we had mastered this we were encouraged to let go one hand and then the other. Once we could float independently we were taught how to propel ourselves in the water from one side to the other, dive under the water to change direction and swim back again. There were certificates for being able to swim 10, 25 and 50 yards. Immersion in cold water was never a pleasure for me and, although I did learn how to swim, I only gained the 10- and 25-yard certificates.

In 1957 it was my final year at St Mary's. It was the year of the eleven-plus exam, the results of which determined the type of secondary school you would attend. We sat three papers, maths, English and intelligence, then came the long wait until the results were sent back to the school. They were read out in front of assembly. Maureen's name was read out, she had passed and then my name was called. I had also passed. I also won some award for getting the highest marks in the school. I couldn't wait to get home and tell Mum and Dad. As soon as school finished I ran all the way home and burst into Dad's shop with just enough breath to exclaim, 'I got a Grammar!' My parents intended for me to go to St Aloysius at Euston if I got a grammar pass or the Brompton Oratory, where Dad had been a pupil, if I got a lesser pass. In light of my excellent result, Sister Austin persuaded my parents to apply to the Sacred Heart Convent at Hammersmith as they were very particular about taking only the brightest children and it had been some years since a girl from St Mary's had been accepted. The Sacred Heart also had a higher cachet than St Aloysius and a high percentage of pupils who went on to university. My parents applied and I went for an interview feeling very apprehensive but must have made all the right responses as I was accepted and I started in September 1957.

Jeannie Rowe (née Searson):

I attended St Charles Primary School in St Charles Square. The school had been bombed, so one corridor just ended in a brick wall. At playtime, we played in the rubble on the bomb site. I don't remember it being a problem. I can't remember if we did any PE, probably because there was nowhere to do it, but on Monday afternoons we always did Scottish dancing in the dining hall. I enjoyed that. There were twins in our class called Michael and Monica Rose. Monica became famous on the Hughie Green show, *Double Your Money*, on Saturday evenings. Michael was my dancing partner.

The school was strict. We learnt the catechism every day. We spent most of our time doing English and maths. At the end of our time at school, all the focus was on the eleven-plus. Every morning, a select group did maths with the head teacher. There was no talking and we worked solidly. In the afternoons, we did English and general knowledge. We wrote essays and learnt grammar. We had special books and were expected to complete a page of each for homework. I also remember studying *Julius Caesar* and can recite some of the speeches to this day. We did a lot of learning by heart. I don't remember doing much history and geography but the reading books we had were full of stories about famous people and mythological tales, so I think our general knowledge was good. Eventually a new school was built around the other side of the square and I spent my last year of primary school in the new building. By this time we had actually moved to Paddington but my mother liked the school so I continued to go to school there.

Charlie Phillips:

In September 1956, I went to St John's School in Clarendon Road. It was a Secondary Modern school. We used to have a caretaker used to come round and light the coal fires. When my school teacher first talked to me, I knew more history than the average kid. One of the things that shocked them when I first came was because they believed we were sub-standard but

I could have sung the Mass in Latin and some of the teachers didn't know how to handle it. My youth employment officer asked me what I wanted to do and I said I wanted to be a naval architect. He looked at me and said, 'You've got a better chance with London Transport or why don't you join the RAF or the Post Office?'

☙ Margaret Stedman (née Riddick):

I was at St Andrew's when Miss Macdonald-Pierce was the headmistress. She was old fashioned and it was like she was still living in the 1920s. She was a force to be reckoned with. Mr Brackley took over as headmaster in my last few months at that school. Mr Lovett the school caretaker used to come in the classroom and make the fire up in the winter because every classroom had a fireplace. He lived in the house next door to the school. We would walk to the church hall in East Row for school dinners and we all had to hold on to a piece of string when the fog was so bad you couldn't see in front of you, so you didn't lose the stragglers. On May Day one year, I was an attendant to the May Queen. We all had long pink satin dresses and Mum would put a bit of lipstick on me. I held on to the lipstick and accidentally put a long streak of lipstick down my dress.

Mr Ragert was the headmaster when I went to Amberley Road School. I remember my parents bought my school uniform at Bradley and Perrins in Harrow Road. Speech day used to be at Friends' House in Edgware Road and Yehudi Menuhin came along one year and gave out the prizes.

♈ Reg Thackeray:

I went to Wornington Road Infants' School. Our teacher, Miss Harris, was a lovely genteel lady. In the afternoon, the curtains were pulled and they would open up beds and we all had to lay down for a rest period for an hour. When I was first taken to Wornington Road School by my mum and sister, by the time they'd got home I was sitting on the doorstep. I'd escaped. One of the women caused trouble in the playground at the infants' school and, one day, my mum had enough of her and laid her out. Fights always ended in a shake of hands and there was no animosity afterwards.

From there I went to Bevington Road Junior School. Mr Gemmill was the headmaster and there was a lovely old woman called Miss Florrie who taught RE and always wore an old rabbit fur coat. I went to Portobello Road School from there. The headmaster, Mr David, was a very small man and the deputy head, Mr Porter, always looked to me like a parrot because he had a beaky nose but he was a very nice man. We did woodwork with Mr Watson, who had a wooden leg. I don't know if he made it himself. The metalwork teacher was Mr Turnbull and we also had a religious instruction teacher, Mr Pyke, and he used to do a drill reading a page and reference number from the Bible and the first one to find it and read out the correct lines would be rewarded with something like a bar of chocolate or bubblegum. I had a very good job as a milk monitor handing out the bottles of milk and when I came home to my mum at dinner time, I always had a few surplus bottles. I always came home for school dinners.

From there I ended up back to Wornington Road School for the upper school in 1963. Mr Phelan, the maths teacher, was a bit sadistic if you didn't do what you were told. I was sitting by the window one day and couldn't help looking out the window. If he caught you, he would rap you across the knuckles. I think he enjoyed it. We went to Barn Elms and the sports ground along Upper Sheen Road where we did cross-country running, which I hated. Where the horses had run, you could lose your boots in the mud and sometimes we had football, which I was useless at. Because I didn't like football, I would kick the ball in my own goal and then they made me a goalkeeper and I let the balls in so they stopped me doing that. I ended up as a linesman.

Before I left school, I was always absent and if I didn't want to go to school, the doctor would come round and I would get a certificate. I would go out with my dad on the lorry to help him do house clearance instead. One day I went back to school and the teacher said, 'Have you recovered, are you feeling better?' and I said, 'I'm feeling so much better', then he said, 'You looked alright last week when I saw you in your dad's lorry.' There was no comeback. I didn't like school at all and I wanted to be out in the world. When I left school in April 1966, I came out the gate and Mr Carter was there and said to me, 'Are you sure you don't want to go on because you've got great potential?' I said, 'No, I want to go out in the world and make money. My ambition is to be a millionaire.'

🌿 Marg Pithers:

I went to Barlby Road School when it was the old building with open fires and outside toilets. Then I went to Hammersmith County after that. My teacher looked at my writing and said, 'You don't write like that, you're going to write like a normal human being,' and we were all taught to write the same way in italics. Hammersmith County was one of the first comprehensives and they were very strict. Boys and girls were separated. The only school trip we ever did was to London Zoo. It was a hot day and they made us all wear our overcoats. As the day was wearing on we were wilting and, when I got home I was so bad my mum took me to hospital and they found out I had heatstroke.

🌿 Roger Rogowski:

I went to St Andrew's School in Bosworth Road. Football was a favourite game at playtime with the basketball posts at the Golborne Road end of the playground acting as goalposts but an overly enthusiastic kick in the direction of the railway line always brought about an early end to the game. Our stray footballs were usually returned to us eventually by passing railway workers. The playground would be regularly enveloped in smoke, which drifted over the wall from the passing trains. There was a gap in the buildings at the Ladbroke Grove end of Wornington Road, which was sometimes populated by small boys with notebooks jotting down the serial numbers on the trains as they rushed by.

Other playground games normally involved a certain amount of running about and good-natured wrestling like British bulldog and other tag-type games, for boys anyway. Girls' games seemed to involve doing something more restrained like skipping, handstands and throwing balls about. There was an annual sports day at the end of each summer term in the playground, which included various running races and a high jump competition involving a portable high jump and a coarse horsehair mat to land on. The children with the highest pain threshold usually won that and I remember one year one boy jumped over in a Western roll before crashing into the thin mat time and again until he was only competing against himself as the bar was positioned higher and higher. Maybe he felt no pain.

Real as opposed to play violence sometimes broke out in the playground in the form of fights when most children would stop what they were doing and rush over to watch the entertainment before the teacher on duty stopped it. Fights sometimes also took place after school outside in the street as we thought there was less likelihood of getting caught and punished, although there were often a group of mums outside the school gate at the end of the school day, which could be guaranteed to put an early stop to any fighting. I'm sure that fighting, among boys at least, was always limited to fist fights and always one to one. I don't remember anyone being kicked while on the ground or being beaten by several boys. I was involved in one after school fight out in the street that I remember, when I landed a lucky punch and my opponent's white shirt was suddenly covered in blood pouring from his nose. Somehow I escaped the cane for that but I was given several periods of detention.

The girls weren't averse to fighting and seemed to be less scrupulous than the boys as I remember a girl coming back from break time one day crying and carrying a chunk of her dark brown hair, which had been pulled out by another girl, and, in one art class when we were entrusted with scissors, one girl stabbed another one in the leg. It wasn't always just fighting though. Very few children qualified at St Andrew's but any 'fatty' or 'four eyes' could expect to be picked on, likewise anyone whose personal hygiene was below the norm was a 'fleabag'. Any arguments or fights were usually soon forgotten about though, and I don't remember any grudges that lasted more than a day.

The other main after-school attraction was the sweet shop opposite the school, which sold small glasses of pop for a penny and, if my mum didn't collect me from school, we played in an area we called the cage, which was diagonally across from the school entrance, in Southam Street. It was another bomb site but this one had been levelled and tarmacked and a wire fence and gate had been installed at the front. Anyway, it was a rare place to play in other than in the street.

Just at the entrance to the playground was a raised flowerbed, which was always filled with beautiful bedding plants in the summer and, at that end of the playground, were the boys' and girls' outside toilets. Although, the toilet wall must have been about 5ft high or so it seemed to me then, because there was no roof on the toilets there was sometimes a bit of a competition among the boys to see who could pee the highest or even over the wall. I'm sure the girls avoided playing anywhere near that wall. The girls' toilet was in the corner of the playground against the railway wall. Even at a young age, we understood that it was no-man's-land, although it was fun to be dared to run in and out of there to make the girls scream.

Smogs were still a problem in winter in the late Fifties and early Sixties, and on those days my mum would wrap a scarf round my head to act as a filter, with instructions not to take it off until I was inside school. My mum's paranoia might have been understandable as my dad worked full-time at a bakery before he joined Limmer and Trinidad in 1957. He used to cycle in all weathers, often in heavy traffic, to and from the bakery and, one winter, it proved too much and he collapsed in the street and was taken to hospital. We were given various vaccinations at school and foul-tasting iron capsules that we were given on a regular basis. We also had regular visits from the nit nurse so, thinking about it, there was quite a lot of medical care at school. Anyway, on one visit the nurse discovered that I had head lice and my mum took charge by washing my hair every day with some special shampoo.

The infants' class at St Andrew's was on the ground floor at the end of the building closest to the entrance to the playground and was led by Miss Bliss. Lessons usually involved a lot of drawing, painting and playing in the sandpit, which was on a large table in the classroom, and we were allowed an organised sleep during the day. The next class up was next door on the ground floor and so on until you got to the road end of the building before being moved to the first floor, when classes started next to headmaster Mr Brackley's office, which overlooked the road, before migrating towards the back of the building for the final two years as the oldest two classes were combined.

We were taken out for school trips from time to time and once went to the Science Museum. At a time when museums seemed stuffy and full of boring glass cases, the children's gallery in the basement was full of interactive displays. There were working models in big glass cases operated by small brass handles on the outside, which we would turn as fast as possible, although the models inside moved at a snail's pace. There was also a booth with doors at either end operated by photoelectric cells, which we all crowded into and out the other side repeating the process several times. Other school trips included a day at the Tower of London. We all climbed the steps of the Monument that day and, as it was one of the tallest buildings in London at the time, the view was much more spectacular then than it is now. One evening before one Christmas, we were taken by coach to Westminster

Central Hall for a schools carol concert, the first time I'd ever been inside such a huge and impressive building.

In the later classes, we were entrusted with inkwells and pens, which were just a nib on a stick. It was a responsible job to be ink monitor, which required a very steady hand. It was also quite a job to get the ink to form words on the page and to avoid getting ink on hands, face, clothes and everywhere else. Being milk monitor was an easier job, handing out the small bottles of milk from the crates, which were sometimes placed by the fire in winter to thaw them out as all of the classrooms had coal fires. The school had a lending library, which operated during some break times in one of the classrooms staffed by other responsible pupils acting as librarians.

I remember being quite bright compared to most children in my class so my parents were a bit dismayed when I failed my eleven-plus in 1964. If the exam had included any subject other than arithmetic, I'm sure I would have passed but I couldn't remember my tables or add up a column of numbers and get the right answer if my life depended on it. My parents didn't want me to go to Isaac Newton School for whatever reason. Holland Park School, one of the new comprehensives, had a very good reputation but they couldn't get me in there. In the end, I went to North Paddington, which had become a comprehensive school two years before, and had its lower school for children in the first to third years, not far from ha'penny steps in Harrow Road and its upper school, for children in the fourth year upward, towards the other end of Harrow Road in Amberley Road. Before the new term started, I was taken by my parents to Bradley and Perrin's in Harrow Road to be kitted out with my first school uniform, including a blazer with the school badge on the breast pocket, school tie, white shirts, scarf and gym and football or rugby kit, which included the old-style football boots. As I was now at big school, I was able to graduate to long trousers for the first time.

It was a different world from being one of the biggest children to being one of the smallest. There were rumours of bullying of the first years but that never happened that I saw. I don't remember the same level of fighting that happened in and around St Andrew's. Although there was the occasional fight, which always drew an enthusiastic crowd. Football was our favourite pastime at playtime or giving someone the bumps, so it was never a good idea to announce your birthday. It was bad enough being given the bumps but sometimes this involved being accidentally dropped to the ground or the helpers leaving their foot in so birthday boy landed on about a dozen toecaps. I often played football a bit too enthusiastically and arrived home more than once with one or other knee in my long trousers torn, which my mum would repair. I was threatened with a return to short trousers if I did it again but that never happened.

Unlike at primary school, there was a school timetable to follow. We had to make sure we were in the correct classroom on time and there was homework to do in the evening. We had some inspiring teachers and, although I can only remember random names now, Mr Morris, our history teacher stands out. Mr Goodhill, our French teacher, mystified us at the start of our first year by only talking to us in French. The science lab was a place of fascination for me with its collection of glass tubes, beakers and flasks and other lab equipment in tall glass-fronted cabinets, on top of which were displayed various stuffed animals under glass domes. Science lessons were often very practical. We learned about basic body parts by dissecting fish, and made a thermometer by heating a glass tube on a Bunsen burner to seal it at one end before blowing a small bowl, filling the thermometer and sealing the other end, then graduating it by first placing the finished thermometer in ice and then in boiling water. Our thermometers were filled with coloured water, not mercury, but we did discover some mercury on the bench one day and thought it amusing to flick it at each other. So keen on science was I that I gave up some of my breaks to help in the lab by tidying away equipment after classes or helping to set up for the next one.

The school also had very good arts and sports departments and we were bussed once a week to Barn Elms playing fields opposite Craven Cottage. Looking back, it seemed to be perpetually cold and very muddy and the leather footballs and rugby balls seemed as heavy as medicine balls. No matter how cold it was, there was a golden rule that we weren't allowed to wear our vests or underpants under our kit, while the teachers always looked warm in their tracksuits. Classes were often taken by the fearsome Mr Macintyre, who was like an early version of Alex Ferguson. Caked in mud at the end of each lesson, we would troop back to a freezing changing room before soaking under boiling hot showers, which filled the changing room with clouds of steam. It was often fun to flick wet towels at each others' bare bottoms for a while before getting dressed and piling back onto the coach with muddy kit rammed into duffel bags to be sorted out later by our mums.

Woodwork classes provided us with the opportunity to use proper tools. We made various small practical items that might be useful at home. We seemed to take an age to make each one, constructed with varying levels of care with mortice and tenon or dovetail joints. I remember proudly taking home a stool, a box for shoe cleaning equipment and a swivelling wall-mounted towel rail, all in my first year.

The Queen paid a visit to both lower and upper schools in 1965 and a video of the event can be seen online on the British Pathé website. I don't feature as I was placed with about a hundred or so other children in the assembly hall to see a presentation to the Queen while other children were placed in the playground to cheer when instructed as she arrived and left.

Mossy Condon:

I went to St Andrew's first, then Isaac Newton. I went to Portobello Road to the lower school for the first two years and then to the upper school in Wornington Road. I played for the football team and, the first year I was there, we won the league and I think it was the first time they'd won the league in about twenty years. We were all brought up on the stage and we were very popular because we had won this big trophy. We all got tiny little medals. My dad took mine to Whiteley's and got it engraved one Saturday and I thought it was the dog's knees, it was so important to me at 12 years of age.

Barbara Reynolds (née Murray):

My favourite teacher at St Andrew's was Miss Bliss, who took the first year's class. In the afternoons, we had to cross our arms on the table and go to sleep. Tony Hunt punched me on the nose one day. Miss Bliss carried me home because I wouldn't stop bleeding. By the time we got to our house, her white blouse was covered in blood and my gran offered to wash it for her.

The boys played at one end of the playground and the girls at the other end, so we used to play lots of girls' games. We would play games like Poor Jenny is a-Weeping, where we used to have a big circle and a girl inside the circle who used to pretend to cry while we sang and certain people would be called into the ring by the girl in the ring. Another game was There Came a Duke a-Riding, where you used to have to do a skip dance.

They used to pull the partition back between two classrooms on the ground floor and that's where we had our morning assembly. We used to stand between the desks and have our assembly and, when they finished, they pulled the partition back to make two classrooms. If we done May Day or the nativity play, they used to stack all the tables and chairs all around the walls. I remember being the Archangel Gabriel one year in the school nativity and I still remember the words to this day. We used to dance round a maypole in the two classrooms on May Day. I was in the church hall one time carrying a purple velvet cushion with a crown on it for the May Queen. It was so heavy, I was afraid to drop it. Everybody used to dress up for that day when the May Queen used to be crowned.

Myself and Robert went to the Albert Hall one time because all the children in the school collected money for Princess Alexandra for the children's charity. We went up there in Mr Brackley's car and we had to go up and give the money to Princess Alexandra. Robert had to bow and I had to curtsy. There were loads of children there from all different schools. It was just me and Robert went from our school.

Bob Crawley:

All three of us children started school life at St Andrew's School on the corner of Bosworth Road and Southam Street. My sister and I stayed at the school until we moved away but my brother was transferred earlier to John Aird School for the blind and partially sighted after it was discovered that his poor attainment at school was due to him not being able to see the blackboard. I was always envious that my brother was taken to and from school in a green bus that collected and delivered him back each day.

I had two stints at St Andrew's School, from about 1958 to about 1961 and then again from about 1963 to 1965 when we returned to Bosworth Road following the demolition of Golborne Gardens and the building of Appleford and Bosworth Houses. I remember Miss Bliss and Mr Brackley but I don't remember any other teachers. During games time, the ball would often go over the playground wall on to the railway line below and you were allowed to climb over the wall at the end of the playground to get the ball under the watchful eye of the teacher. We used to go from St Andrew's School to St Thomas' Church hall for school dinners and we went past the Catholic school. They were in red and white uniforms and we didn't have a uniform. We thought they were all Irish Catholics. It was like there was a bit of segregation between of us and them. We went to Heathrow Airport with the school one afternoon and I took my Brownie camera to take photos of the VC10s taking off and coming in but when the film came back, they were like pin pricks in the sky, so you could hardly make them out. Heathrow was still being developed and we could walk wherever we liked.

I then went to North Paddington School in Harrow Road. I was interviewed by Mr Davies with my mum before I went to the school. It was more of an informal chat. He said, 'We play rugby.' I said, 'I wear glasses all the time.' He said, 'That won't be a problem. Take them off.' The problem was they would throw the ball at me and I couldn't see a thing. I was in the football team wearing my glasses and kept breaking them. I hated games. You were only allowed to wear a v-necked, short-sleeved shirt and shorts with nothing underneath and, if your gear was dirty from the day before, they would slipper your arse and that stung. You're freezing cold and the teachers are in tracksuits. You'd have a shower afterwards and you couldn't use your hands because they were so cold.

The thing I remember there was the violence. One of the teachers hit a kid with a bit of four by two. Some of the boys tried to hang a kid off one of the basketball posts in the playground, tied him by his feet and threw a rope over and dragged him up for a laugh. The ringleader got caught and started having a row with the teacher, so the teacher hit him and told him to get out the school and he was expelled. One of the teachers pushed a kid through a window. A kid turned up and didn't want to do games and got slippered. His mum, a violent woman, came to the school and had a go at the teacher. The next week we are doing PT and the kid said, 'I haven't got my kit.' The teacher said, 'Are you going to get your mum?' They had a row and the teacher pushed the kid, who went through a glass screen. The teacher said to us, 'You all saw what happened didn't you? It was an accident.' There was never any comeback. Girls used protractors on other girls and fought as bad as the boys. A couple of kids always got the cane and it seemed to make no difference to them.

One of the boys in my class, Clyde, who went on to become a deputy headmaster in a London school, was playing around with bromides in chemistry class and had to go to hospital to have his stomach pumped. Mr Heath was the maths teacher. He lived in Hither Green and took the 36 bus home. You weren't allowed to write anything down unless he said. He was in absolute control of his class. He had a very good success rate in getting kids through their GCE. A lot of kids went on to have good careers. One kid went on to play the piano in the London Junior Symphony Orchestra and appeared on TV. When we did woodwork at North Pad, we built canoes and they chose a few of us to test them out on the canal, which was at the back of the school. It sounds dangerous but Mr Greenwood, the woodwork teacher, made sure there was no problem.

I remember the Queen's visit. We had a competition to paint a portrait of the Queen. It was on cardboard-type paper and mine was chosen as one of the pictures to present to the Queen. We were told not to put our heads up and to speak only when spoken to. She came into our classroom and everyone started staring. She made polite conversation with some of the kids. We were late out of school that day because they locked the gates until the Queen left. The school had been painted probably for the first time in living memory.

Christine Smith:

When I was 4 years old, I was taken down to St Mary's School in East Row, to meet the headmistress, Sister Mary Anselm, who interviewed my father and put me on the register to start at the school in January 1960. School was an enormous shock to the system. For the first few days I never took my coat or bright red beret off and sat like a stone in Class 1 with a tall skinny teacher called Miss Kenny. I was horrified that I was left there. Unlike today with crèches, nurseries or half day at school, we all started full time immediately. Eventually I began to copy the others, who were playing with various toys, but we actually started to learn to read and write in Year 1 and my mother proudly boasted that I could read and write within six months.

The school was run by the Sisters of Mercy, who used to arrive in a chauffeured car each morning. Both headmistresses, Sister Mary Anselm in the infants and Sister Mary Austin in the juniors, ran their units with a rod of iron. There were lay teachers too but it was a very strict place and I was very relieved when I finally left it in 1966 to go to my secondary school in Willesden. I used to collect my friend, Susan, from Ruth House in Kensal Road on the way to school. We used to come from the crossing at St John's in Harrow Road, over the bridge into Kensal Road, past the old dust yard on the left by the canal and then into East Row. The school backed onto the bus garage and the workers there were forever throwing all the balls down into the playground from their roof to us. There were very few families with only one or two children. The average was four or five but I was in a class with one girl who was from a family of fourteen and she also had two cousins living with them. I was also asked to take a younger child to school from Kensal Road. There were some houses that were very run-down and her house had no hot water, bath or amenities.

I wrote an essay at school describing 'What I did at the weekend', but it was considered fantasy when I described being driven about in a black taxi cab. No one, teacher or other pupils believed me until my Uncle George took me down to the church in Bosworth Road for my Confirmation in 1966 in his black cab.

 *Brian Collins:*

I started in the infants' school in Treadgold Street and, when I was 7, I went to an all-boys' junior school and then to Cardinal Manning. When I was at junior school, we were taught racist songs by the older boys. You'd be the youngest in the school at 7 years old and it was put into your mind that black people lived in a certain way, mocking them. I remember a song that we were made to learn that started, 'We no work but we get fat, eating our daily Kit-e-Kat.' One of my best friends, who lived round the corner in Wilsham Street, was mixed race so there was that tension that some boys were saying horrible things and we were the best of friends.

Susan Mcmahon:

I went to Bevington before we moved then I went to Queen's Park after we moved. One day soon after I started at Bevington, I thought, 'I don't like it,' so I just walked out and went home. I knew my way back home because there were no gates or alarms in those days.

seven

Shopping

✿ Jane Traies:

On my way to school, I would go past Green's, the little shop on the corner of St Lawrence's Terrace, and say hello to Mrs Green. Once my mum was too busy to come out the shop so she sent me up to Mrs Green's to buy a packet of sanitary towels. You couldn't say it out loud in those days, so she wrote it on a bit of paper and gave it to me and said, 'Go and give this to Mrs Green,' so I gave the bit of paper to Mrs Green, who gave me a great big conspiratorial wink as one woman to another and she gave me this big packet that she wrapped in newspaper so it couldn't be seen when I walked back, and she said, 'There you are, give that to your mum.'

After the war when we were very little, those shops in Golborne Road were a real community. The other shopkeepers were always introduced to us as uncle, so it was Uncle Henry Holm at the bakers, Uncle Dai Williams at the chemist, Uncle Trevor Edwards in the dairy and they would all end up in the Carnarvon after they all closed up. Going down the street, there was Price's, then Taverner's, then the toyshop, then the butchers, then Dai Williams the chemist, Edwards the dairy, then the corner of Portobello and Golborne where the eel man had his stall on Friday and Saturday. The eels were in a tank. If you bought one they would fetch it out the tank and chop it up while it still wriggled. It was revolting but we were fascinated by that.

Ella, Henry's sister, was Meyer but Henry called himself Henry Holm. Ella Meyer did a lot of the selling at the top shop and Henry did the baking. It was the first place I ever saw a machine for slicing bread. Granny remembered when they let people bring their turkeys in to cook them in the gas ovens at Christmas because their ovens at home weren't big enough. They used to have the most elaborate cakes for celebrations in the window. We used to stand for ages looking at the cakes.

My granny bought me a scooter in Harper's toyshop for my 7th birthday. It was toys upstairs at Harper's and records downstairs. In the flat above the pawn shop on the corner of Bevington Road, exactly opposite us in Golborne Road, was a very old lady called Ada Louise and we were told she had been in the music halls. She used to wash her hair and hang it out the window to dry.

Our Uncle Norman Traies had a shop selling pianos in Portobello Road. Portobello always had divisions. There was the scruffy jumbly end near Golborne Road. There were the antiques at the top and the bit selling fruit and veg in the middle. There was the man under the bridge selling china and textiles with the patter. How he didn't smash those plates I don't know. There was a Midland Bank on the corner where the antiques started, where the

Portobello market with the Imperial, known by almost everyone at the time as the bug'ole, in the background, 1969. Its proximity to the fruit and vegetable stalls provided small boys with useful ammunition if the film broke down or became too boring.

Golborne Road market at the junction with Bevington Road, 1967. Second-hand goods were on the south side of the road and all other goods on the north side, a traditional that more or less still holds today.

posh end started up to the Sun in Splendour. After the market, on Saturday night, poor families used to wheel their prams along the road and pick up all the vegetables left behind in the gutter.

Margaret Burdsey (née Traies):

There was a shop further up from us towards the iron bridge we called 'the help yourself'. It was called the Economic Grocer. It was like an early supermarket. You just helped yourself to the tins on the shelf. There were two strange dress shops with plastic bodices in the window with beige bras and short-sleeved tops, and that's where we were bought our liberty bodices when we were young. They had rubber buttons so they could go through the mangle. I remember the pie and mash shop but we never went there because our mum was a good cook and she thought it was a bit common.

Later on, when we moved to Golborne, it was a great time. The market was there on Saturday. There was music playing. There was a dress shop up by the Mitre where I got a lovely check suit, which I wore for interviews. We thought we were blessed because we were growing up close to Portobello Road in the Swinging Sixties and they were our formative years. It was a wonderful time as a teenager. By then, Portobello Road sold tie-dye shirts. My mum was horrified when I bought a skirt on one of the ex-military stalls like one she wore when she was in the WAAF and I'd spent money on it.

❧ *Pauline Clark (née Harding):*

Mum would send me over the butcher's over the ha'penny steps to Harrow Road to get the meat every day before I went to school. It was hard when we had ration books. There were so many things we couldn't get. I would go shopping down the lane, mainly on a Saturday afternoon. There were all totters' barrows along there. I would be given a list of shopping at the end of the week and I would struggle home.

∼ *Maureen Rafferty (née Coker):*

My mum would go straight up the Golborne to shops like Hamperl's the butcher and get things like pease pudding and saveloys, and Holm's for bread. All the shopping was local. The cockle lady at the far end of Golborne was another place to stop. There was a shop that used a wire to cut the cheese and we used to go in to Clarke's for fishing bait.

❦ *Derek Ford:*

My mum would go shopping down the Golborne and Saturdays she would meet up with my grandmother and go down the Portobello Road, which my nan used to call the lane. She would always say, 'We're going up the lane.' She always referred to London around Leicester Square as 'up west'; 'We're going up west.' I used to go up Golborne to get my records at Harper's, haircuts at Roe's and the Greeks' fish and chip shop by the bridge.

Alan Warner:

Whenever coal was needed, it was me who had to go over the Town to the coal yard and get 28lb of nutty slack, which was bits of coal with plenty of dust. That was a horrible journey coming back with that sack.

Gwen Nelson (née Martin):

Even though Dad had the grocery shop, there were still items that had to be bought elsewhere. We always bought full cream milk which came in a glass bottle. In those days milk wasn't homogenised and the cream would separate out and float to the top to be carefully decanted and kept aside to go on top of the evening's pudding.

Just as you crossed the bridge, on the right-hand side was the Greek fish and chip shop with a high counter with jars of gherkins and pickled eggs on it. Further down was Clarke's, which was a corn chandlers and sold bird seed to the pigeon fanciers in the district and hay and oats to the totters whose ponies were stabled in Munro Mews or Hazlewood Crescent. On that side there was also a Methodist chapel and a dress shop. On the left-hand side, by St Ervans Road was a newsagents. To access it, you had to go down steep iron steps to a little courtyard and the shop was tucked away under the bridge. It was known as Slider's but I don't know if that was the name of the shop or the steps as a result of what people became in wet or frosty weather.

Until Mum had her own shop in the late 1950s, she worked full-time with Dad so, from about 7 or 8 years old, I was the one who did the shopping. Saturday morning, Mum would give me a 10s note to buy a joint and vegetables for the weekend. I'd take my shopping bags down to Cullingford's, the butcher the other side of the iron bridge, and to Price's the greengrocers. The first time I went, the butcher refused to believe that Mum had given me the money and wouldn't serve me so I had to backtrack and get a note from Mum. After that they knew me and would often make suggestions about different cuts of meat they thought we might like. A half leg of lamb was a favourite for Sunday lunch. Other delicacies which have long since vanished from butchers included sweetbreads, brains, tripe and sheep's and beef heart. Sweetbreads and brains would be dipped into beaten egg and rolled in flour before being deep fried. Tripe was cooked in milk with chopped onion and then thickened with butter and flour. The hearts would be stuffed with a mix of breadcrumbs, herbs and chopped onion before being casseroled in Bisto gravy. The other butcher along the Golborne was Hamperl's, which sold pease pudding and faggots and other takeaway food. There was always a queue. You had to bring your own container and the pease pud was ladled into it from steaming vats.

Price's was a treasure trove. The basics, fruit and vegetables, were on display outside on sloping racks but inside there were exotic fruits such as pomegranates and bananas. I'd pick the potatoes, carrots and parsnips, which were all put into brown paper bags I had with me. No such thing as pre-washed vegetables then but they stayed fresher longer than today's supermarket produce. A cabbage or cauliflower and a couple of Granny Smith's would be the last of my purchases and then it was the long walk home. A shopping trip down Golborne was never complete without a stop in Holm's bakery. Like Hamperl's, Holm's was originally owned and run by a German family. Holm's sold the most delicious selection of cakes and my Saturday mission was to buy three apple turnovers and three lemon curd tarts for lunch as well as miniature Hovis loaves that were made on the premises.

Saturday was also pocket money day and, once I'd dropped off the shopping, I was free to go my own way with my money. Sometimes this was up to Woolworths in Harrow Road, where I became very proficient in helping myself to pick and mix samples before I made my actual purchase. Other times I would wander down the lane, as Portobello Road was known. One of my favourite stalls was the one that sold second-hand books. Even sixty years later I still have a few that I bought, including *The Yellow Fairy Book* by Andrew Lang with its beautiful illustrations by Henry Ford.

On the same side as Holm's in Golborne Road was Harper's record shop. Mum and I would listen to the radio during the week and on Saturday I would go in with a list of records to buy. Lita Roza singing 'How Much is that Doggie in the Window?' was an early purchase, as was 'Rock Around the Clock' by Bill Haley and the Comets, Tommy Steele's 'Little White Bull', 'Sixteen Tons' by Tennessee Ernie Ford and many more. I'd buy three or four records at a time and by the end of my Saturday shop, felt as if I was lugging home 16 tons myself.

꒰ Charlie Phillips:

When I first came here, you could get a pig head, oxtail or spare ribs for free. Just tell the butcher you got a dog. The only rice dishes you could get was rice pudding but that all changed later. When we first came here, the only choice of fashion we had was black, navy blue or grey but then our fashion came later based on styles like the zoot suit. Old cockney families like the Cains and the Prices and the old pie and mash in Portobello Road served the community. They were like institutions. I used to help the Prices sometimes with their barrow in the mews. Our local butcher's, Mr Walters at the top end of Portobello Road, started to properly cater for the Afro-Caribbean community, selling things like oxtails and pig heads. He later sold up and went to Israel. In All Saints Mews, I used to go and buy paraffin. Up in St Ervans Road there used to be a big coal yard and, to make extra pocket money, I used to have an old pram and run errands for old ladies, especially Mrs Ward in Portobello Road. I would buy a bag of coal and she would give me sixpence for delivering it.

꒰ Margaret Stedman (née Riddick):

I bought my first portable record player from Harper's. My first record was Elvis Presley. I wore it out I played it so much. I then bought a stereo radiogram from Turner's in Portobello Road. What a piece of furniture that was! I worked at Marks & Spencer's in Hammersmith and every Friday on the way home I would go in and pay money off for the record player. I bought my first pram in Golborne Road at Harper's.

꒰ Reg Thackeray:

Paraffin was two and six a gallon and you could buy it from O'Mahoney's and Hibberd's in Golborne Road, and a man also used to go round selling it so you could buy it in the street. The market was always Friday and Saturday. Second-hand wasn't allowed on the north side, always new on that side. On the north side of Golborne, there was Joe Francis first with fruit and veg, then Georgie Lanson with flowers, then Tommy Mason with seafood, then the man with cakes and eggs, then another fruit and veg, then Cissie and Teddy Price; Price's had three stalls outside their shop, one fruit, one veg and one all salad. They used to have big lights with globes on. They didn't have electric out to the road then. After that there was a man who always had a camel hair overcoat on who used to sell comics like *Casper the Friendly Ghost*, *Richie Rich* and *Superman*. You'd buy them and when you'd read them you'd take them back, pay a bit more and buy another one, so he sold new and second-hand. After that, there was a stall selling nylon stockings and ladies underwear, and then more fruit and veg. Hamperl's the butcher was famous for its faggots and pease pudding. There was a mechanical model pig with a tray in the window that used to move from side to side. Mrs Holm's daughter married the Hamperls' son. The Holm family lived above the bakery.

🌿 Marg Pithers:

In the Portobello Road, there was a material store and there was an actress who lived locally, Rita Webb. She made her own clothes and you would hear her effing and blinding when they came to the price. There was a dress shop in Golborne Road. I bought a dress in there one day. You couldn't try dresses on in there and, when I got home, I could have fitted two of me inside. They wouldn't give me my money back so my mum went up there and got it. She must have been in there half an hour. She slapped the money in my hand and said, 'Don't buy anything else in there.'

🐦 Roger Rogowski:

Mum went shopping every day and the first stop was almost always Vic Martin's grocery shop in Golborne Road. Holm's the baker, on the left over the iron bridge, was usually the next stop, followed by Price's the greengrocer further down Golborne Road on the right-hand side, and then Hamperl, the butcher on the same side back towards the iron bridge. Chicken was a relatively expensive meat then and turkey almost unknown, so chicken was always a Christmas treat in our house. One year on Christmas Eve, my dad returned from shopping, as there was probably some heavy lifting to do, and said he was sure that we had the winning raffle ticket displayed in Hamperl's window. Mum and Dad hunted high and low for the raffle ticket and finally found it at the bottom of the kitchen bin, a bit smelly and crumpled but readable and Dad struggled home later with our prize 20lb turkey, which they had to cut the legs off to fit in the oven.

There were stalls selling fresh fruit, veg and other food on one side of Golborne Road over the iron bridge and second-hand clothes stalls on the other side. Around the corner in Portobello Road close to the railway bridge, there was also usually a large van piled high with towels, bedding, crockery, pots and pans and other household goods, which often drew a crowd while the seller put on a performance along the lines of, 'I'm not asking for a pound, I'm not even asking for ten bob, move closer madam. Look at the quality, I'm giving them away here, two for ten bob.'

❧ Bob Crawley:

All the shopping in our family was done by my mum or, for odd items, my sister or I were dispatched to the local shop, in our case, Jones' Dairy at the junction of Bosworth Road and Kensal Road. Bigger needs were met by shops in Golborne Road at David Greig's, Home and Colonial and latterly Tesco's and the local butchers and greengrocers, of which there were several, not forgetting the barrows that were out. Christmas shopping for clothes was extended to Kensington High Street, mainly C&A, and on the odd occasion to Oxford Street. An occasional foray was made to Harrow Road and I recall that our school uniform for North Paddington had to be obtained from an outfitters designated by the school in Harrow Road at considerable cost compared to other shops.

I remember the greengrocers using scales with brass weights and, when buying potatoes, they would adjust the weight by removing or adding small potatoes to get to the correct weight. In Jones' Dairy in Kensal Road, you had to wait behind the other shoppers while Mr Jones went and fetched each item, including slicing ham, cheese and spam and so on, wrote the price down in a list and then mentally added up the total. Very personal service but slow, just like *Open All Hours* with Ronnie Barker. Mr Jones was also a local milkman who delivered before he opened the shop in the morning. In later years, and in a shop just down from the dairy, was a newsagent where secondary school-age kids could buy threepenny loose cigarettes and have a quick smoke on the way to school. In those days cigarettes were also sold in fives but still cost too much for schoolkids.

 *Brian Collins:*

My mum liked Shepherd's Bush market. We would go along there through Norland market. There was a toyshop there where I might get a treat on the way back. Closer to home, in the late Fifties virtually through the Sixties, there weren't any supermarkets so you went to the local shops. Our local shops were Scotty's and Holland's Dairy run by a Welsh family in Portland Road and that's where you got your milk and eggs. You went to the butchers and the bakers and there were hardware shops where you would get paraffin for your heaters and drawer liners, which my mum was quite fussy about. Shops would sell glasses of drink for a penny and threepence of loose cigarettes.

You could pay money every week into your firework fund and on November the fifth you would go in and the lady would say you've paid in ten bob over the course of the year so you can have ten bobs' worth of fireworks. There were some people who were a bit hard up so shops would allow them to get things on tick and pay up on payday. The lady who ran Shepherd's was very nice like that. It was probably the least used shop in the area because it didn't seem to stock much compared to places like Carol-Ann's, Scotty's or Tedder's. My mum would sometimes say 'We're out of something, go up to Shepherd's,' because they would stay open until really late and she would give me two bob. The lady wouldn't be in the shop. She would be out the back watching telly. I would go in there and call out and she would sometimes say, 'We don't have change for two bob, can you go across to the Portland?' As a 7- or 8-year-old, I would go into the off-licence side and ask them for change. It was embarrassing, it really was.

We would go to Portobello market in the afternoon because they had all the veg and things like bacon. Past the fruit and veg bit, under the bridge, there was the junk part of the market. There was a bloke on the corner called Jock who sold all sorts of weird stuff. My dad loved rummaging through the junk looking for bargains. He was a hard-working man and my mum was a cleaner but he had seven children to bring up so he was always on the lookout for a bargain. We'd make our way up to Golborne to pick up a few things and I'd have a look in the window of Harper's and see a toy I'd like when I get my pocket money. We'd walk back through Portobello Road and that would take us up to teatime.

✿ Susan Mcmahon:

On a Friday or Saturday, my mum would take me down Portobello and she would talk to everybody for hours. She would start at Golborne and then round the corner to Portobello Road where the rag stalls were and used to look at every stall. Then she would work her way up to the top and buy all her fruit and veg. She would take hours and I would be begging her to take me home.

eight

Social Life

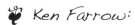 *Ken Farrow:*

My mum took me down the bug'ole in Portobello Road and the Coliseum in Harrow Road. They were both on a par, sixpence to get in and scratch all night. We saw some fantastic films. My stepbrother took me one time to see a film called *The Runaway Bus* starring Frankie Howerd. We rolled laughing all the way home. I've seen it since and I don't know what was so bloody funny. Saturday afternoon matinee was a bus ride away, so that was a bit more expensive. We would go to the ABC Club on Saturday morning matinee at the Prince of Wales in Harrow Road next to the police station. Sometimes we went to the Royalty but sometimes they showed the same films. If I went to the ABC Club, I would still have to go shopping afterwards.

Where the lamp post is now in front of Hazlewood Tower in Golborne Road was a stink pipe for the sewer or a ventilation pipe of some kind. It was tall and quite a landmark. On a Friday evening, all the local racing pigeon owners would meet at Wornington Road School, Florence Gladstone as it later became. The birds would be registered and ringed with special rubber rings and put in crates that would be dispatched to some distant place, like Cornwall, Scotland and even France. At a specified time, the local railway staff would release the birds and the race would be on. Back home, as the time drew near, the fanciers would wait, usually inside their lofts, for the pigeons to arrive. The ring would be removed and then someone would have to run with it to the clock by the stink pipe at the top of Hazlewood Crescent. This had all been handicapped of course to allow for the different distances as some, like my stepdad, were only around the corner, whereas others might be as far away as the Portobello or Ladbroke Grove. Seconds were critical and it didn't pay to get in the way of the runner or you could end up in hospital, especially if, like my brother, you had to run through the house.

When I was older, I drank in the Brit on the corner of Kensal and Golborne with a couple of friends who lived Latimer Road way. They would sometimes try to get me drunk lining up gin and tonics on the bar but they didn't have any effect. We might start up a pub crawl and end up in Harlesden, Willesden, the Scrubs, Acton. We'd take the glass with us and put it in our pockets. The Arthur was Irish so we never went in there. You wouldn't have any trouble but you could guarantee there would be a fight just for the sake of having a fight before the end of the evening, so we stayed out.

Later on there were some pubs that were blacks only. It wasn't just nationalities. Sometimes it would be class. There were navvies' pubs where you could go in in your work clothes on the way home from work but when you went out in the evening in your best clothes you went to other pubs. The Brit was a bit of a cut above. There were fights in there sometimes

The Riddick family, with Margaret Stedman (nee Riddick) in the foreground, outside the Apollo in All Saints Road, 1953. This view would be fairly recognisable today. The Apollo closed in 1983 and is now multi-use business units.

Golborne Road shopkeepers at the Kensal Rise Constitutional Club, 1949. Back row: Mr Holm Senior (baker), Johnny Taverner, Trevor Edwards (dairy), Dai Williams (chemist). Middle row: Jack Taverner (newsagent), Reenie Taverner, Ray Davidson, unknown couple, Blake Traies (newsagent), Audrey Edwards, Teddy Davidson. Front row: Lionel Smith, Floss Williams, unknown woman, Edna Holm, Henry Holm, Phyl Davidson, Ella Holm.

but usually there was no trouble. One night I grabbed a girl's beehive and pulled her hair and nothing happened. On Christmas Eve you would go round and kiss every girl in the pub and some of them would come after you to kiss. You could start at the Brit, then go to the Derby, then the Forester's, then the Lads, up the steps to the Cowshed. Sometimes we never got out of Kensal Road and sometimes we never got out of the Brit.

Dennis Smith:

There was a cider house in Harrow Road. Everyone was fighting. There was fights in most pubs but they were just friendly fights. There was a pub we called the little house in West Row right next to Simmons's yard. They used to sell beer and spirits but they would have to get the beer in the basement so, if you went in there and ordered, say, a scotch and a beer, they would give you your scotch and go down in the basement to fetch the beer. By the time they'd come back, you'd drunk the scotch and gone down the road with about four bags of crisps as well. I was 16 or 17 when I was in the Forester's one time having a game of darts. All of a sudden, a copper looked in the door and said, 'You, outside.' The governor came out and said to the copper, 'I've seen his birth certificate. He's 18.'

Jane Traies:

Thursday afternoon was half day closing and Mum and Dad would go to Kensington High Street shopping. They might go to Barker's or Whiteley's. My dad was disabled because he lost a leg in the war, so he had a car quite early. He would drive us up to the City of London on a Sunday afternoon after the shop was closed and we would walk around and they would point out a bomb site and say, 'Before the war that was there.' That was a brilliant day out just to see London. He wouldn't give up, our dad. He stood behind that counter for thirty or forty years on that wooden leg and they were primitive in those days. He was in such pain sometimes.

Margaret Burdsey (née Traies):

Despite dad's disability, we used to go down to Wormwood Scrubs on a Sunday afternoon. Sometimes we'd get a tennis court, sometimes we'd just run about. He came swimming with us sometimes. He would come swimming in the evening, which was quite a surprise because he didn't want people to see him with his artificial leg. Mum would say to us, 'You must tell your friends your dad is going to take his leg off,' because she thought they would be so shocked but they weren't shocked at all. He could move in the water better than he could walk. He was a wonderful swimmer. As children, we walked down to the rec in St Mark's Park from Ladbroke Grove because we could walk down there on our own.

We used to go on an outing on Ascension Day. We had a day off from school on that day. We would put our uniforms on and walk up to Kensal Rise station from Ladbroke Grove to Parliament Hill Fields, Gospel Oak, and we had a lovely day there, although most of the day was spent travelling there and back. We played with our friends and ate our picnic. I remember it as a good day out, something to look forward to each year.

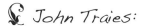 John Traies:

My dad and grandad were Masons, so their social life revolved around that. My dad worked six and a half days a week, six to six, so he didn't have much time for a social life. By evening time, he was whacked. They used to invite friends round for a drink and they used to go to the Constitutional Club in Chamberlayne Road off Kensal Rise. My dad wasn't a pub man but my grandad was. He would go over to the Carnarvon after he closed his shop. If we wanted our grandad after the shop had closed, we had to go in there.

My whole social life revolved around football, going to watch it or playing. We would often go down to Wormwood Scrubs to play cricket or football in the evening. Why I became such a good goalkeeper, dad would pivot on his good leg and fire these balls in with his wooden leg at about 100 miles an hour. I first went to QPR in 1962 when Bill Protheroe took me, so I would have been 9, and then we went to White City for a year in 1963 then back to Loftus Road. There was a running track at White City, so you could hardly see the pitch. I went to a QPR game with my sister Margaret and her boyfriend. Mark Lazarus missed the goal and the ball came into the crowd. I put my little hand out and the ball bent my thumb right back and I broke my thumb. My sister sent me home on my own on the tube all the way from Shepherd's Bush to Ladbroke Grove and my mum didn't half give her some stick when she got in.

The Rodney Marsh years were such a fantastic time to go in the mid- to late Sixties. Parents were calling their baby boys Rodney. I walked to and from Wembley on that magical day with my mate David Thomas. We stood behind the goal where all five goals went in. It was our greatest day, coming back from 2-0 down to win 3-2. It was trendy to go to Rangers. Carol White the actress used to go. We won the Third Division and then got promoted from the Second Division. Ron Springett, Johnny Collins and Mike Keen used to come and coach at Clement Danes because it was only across the way, so you would get the England goalkeeper to shoot the ball at. I had all the old programmes but my mum made me give them to my godson. I wish I still had them.

Derek Ford:

From the age of 7 to 10 I was going down Queens Park Rangers on my own. I'd go round the corner by the Earl Percy into Ladbroke Grove, down to the station, on the train to Shepherd's Bush. Bear in mind a night match would finish about quarter past nine. My dad used to take me there when I was the age of 3, 4 and 5 but I don't recall anything before 5. I sometimes went to Fulham too. I was a football fanatic. My claim to fame is that I once saw three matches in one day. I went to QPR at eleven o'clock, then Brentford at three and then shot over on the Met Line to West Ham for a seven thirty, bear in mind how young I was.

Richard Rowlands:

They would get a crate of beer on a Saturday round here and have a party, and that would be it. No one would go to work on a Monday. There used to be a café, the El Portobello. If you come out of Acklam Road, there used to be a pub on the corner and it was a few shops down from there. We all used to meet in there and take a few purple hearts and then go up the West End, early Sixties, about 1964. We used to take ten and you wouldn't come home until Wednesday. We would go up the Whisky-A-Go-Go and different gaffs. It would be fantastic. We would see Georgie Fame, Eric Burdon, Chris Farlowe, Zoot Money, all them old-time singers.

Our local thing was to walk up Queensway and go in the Golden Egg by where Whiteley's was. We never stopped laughing. We did everything for a laugh. I never had a fight in me life. I would turn it into a joke but my brother was in and out of prison for fighting. All we've ever done is laughed but the ones before us, all they've done is fought, in wars and all that.

Gwen Nelson (née Martin):

At the back of Golborne Road, running between Edenham and Southam Streets, was the Seven Feathers, a youth club. Alcohol was forbidden but despite this it was very popular with teenagers. From our upstairs back windows we could watch the activities and listen to the music coming from the club. For adults there were several choices of where to go of an evening or on the weekend. There were several cinemas. Closest were the Prince of Wales on Harrow Road and the Imperial on Portobello Road, popularly known as the bughole.

The Prince of Wales was an impressive art deco building with cream tiles and three very tall windows facing the street. It had a large entrance foyer and people would queue for tickets. No pre-booking in those days. You just turned up, paid yer money and took yer chances. When all the seats had been taken a 'full' notice would be put up but some people were still admitted and stood at the back behind the seats waiting for a seat as one came empty. This happened quite frequently as films were shown on a continuous loop and often you'd arrive midway through the supporting picture or the Pathé News. People would get up and leave as the picture reached the part where they'd come in, so there was a constant flux.

The Imperial was a shabby, do-it-yourself affair. Its façade was coated with what were once white tiles but were now cracked and stained and covered with faded posters advertising films shown weeks, if not months earlier. Inside was dilapidated with rows of hard wooden seats, frequently missing a vital part such as a seat or back. It was dark, damp and called the bughole for the practical reason that it was common to exit a performance covered in bites and scratching furiously. Management was minimal and one of the joys, particularly for the boys who went there, was to throw rotten fruit if the picture failed to hold their attention. Its position in Portobello Road facilitated the acquisition of rotten fruit left by the traders after they'd closed their stalls.

There were pubs aplenty. Opposite us was the Prince Arthur and on the corner of Southam Street, the Earl of Warwick, while over the iron bridge was the Mitre. Although Dad rarely frequented the Arthur, he was on good terms with the licensee, as he was with all the other shopkeepers on the block, and they had an amicable arrangement about purchasing goods from each other. At Christmas, Dad would be given a box of a dozen assorted bottles of spirits as a goodwill gesture. Neither he nor my mum drank a great deal as both had a very poor head for alcohol, so most of it was given away as presents to relatives. Most pubs had darts teams. For a while in my late teens, I was a member of the Robin Hood and Little John's ladies' team.

In Kensal Road was the Cobden Club. Although not regulars, Mum and Dad would go along on a Saturday night if there was a good act on. Most Saturday nights there would be one of the up and coming young singers, or a semi-retired music hall act. Dad closed the shop at six and had a quick wash and change while mum was cooking dinner and off they'd go, leaving me with a big bag of sweets and the telly. No such thing as a babysitter. I had to lock the lounge door so the gentlemen visitors for the tart upstairs couldn't get in and they'd left a bucket so I didn't have to risk going downstairs to the communal lavatory. There was only one occasion I was frightened and I dressed in my school uniform of grey pleated skirt, golden blouse and red cardigan and made my way, on a very cold, wet night, to the Cobden Club, where I wailed my story to the doorkeeper. Mum and Dad were fetched and, in a less than happy frame of mind because their evening out had been brought to an abrupt close, they took me home and put me to bed.

Sundays were often taken up with sport. Dad was a member of the Kensal Cricket Club despite the infirmities he had as a result of war injuries. What he lacked in ability he made up for in enthusiasm and it was a standing joke in the club that he'd probably be out for a duck. The club's home grounds were at Northolt, which was some distance to travel but easy enough by Central Line. Many of the local lads were team members, Dave Fisher from Golborne Road; his friend Albert; Mike who lived locally; Dave Parsons from off Harrow Road; Bunny Miller, who had been in the RAF and was now chauffeur for a Hatton Garden diamond merchant. In the late 1950s, two West Indians, Roy and his friend whose name I forget, joined the team. Most matches were played against other local teams, either home or away, and wives, sisters and sweethearts would pack individual lunches. One trip we all enjoyed was when Kensal was playing the team from Meopham on their home pitch. Meopham is a small village in Kent, on the North Downs, and cricket was played on the village green in front of two pubs, the King's Arms and the Long Hop. Meopham was so different from living conditions in North Kensington with its picture postcard houses and open spaces.

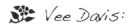 *Vee Davis:*

We used to have loads of parties in what they used to call the Calypso Club in Ledbury Road, right down in the basement. I used to go to nightclubs, the shebeens and the little dens they used to have down in the basements of Notting Hill. As soon as the weekend come, you just party. You buy a top or a skirt or whatever and you look good and you just party until Monday morning and you go back to work. There was so few of us that we were having fun. When we meet each other, we were so happy to be together and party the night away. I come in in the morning when I'm tired. I come in when I had enough.

I had no relatives here, that's why I never took up drinking. I could go to these clubs and I always used to think to myself, 'I don't want to drink because it will go to my head.' Then the next morning I'll wonder, 'How you get in here, what did you do last night?' I don't want to have to worry about that, because I'm a lone woman. Some people were lucky enough to have an auntie, an old aunt or uncle they could call on. Once, there was a place right off the Tabernacle, a Bajan man used to run it, Bajy. They used to have some real rocking music there. On a night I remember being down there and the police raided. They said 'Everybody stand still' and then they came around and they were finding all the drugs on the floor. Everybody drop what they had. Some of them were arrested but I remember going home because they say, after they kept it quiet and they search around, 'You can go.'

Charlie Phillips:

A place my dad used to go was what we called the pisshouse pub. When you look back, that was a community centre because a lot of people went there to meet. I used to wait for my dad outside. My dad went to the pub but my mum wasn't much of a drinker. He would give me a shandy. There was a few of us kids outside. The Electric cinema, we used to call the bughouse. My favourite time was to go there on a Sunday because they would show new films. Someone would come round the back and you would let them in through the back door.

We had a lot of shebeens in people's houses because we weren't very welcome at places like the Lyceum or the Hammersmith Palais, so we had nowhere to go. We didn't want to dance to Victor Sylvester or Joe Loss. There's nothing wrong with their music but we didn't want to foxtrot or do the waltz. We wanted to boogie, so someone would have a sound system and some imported records from Jamaica. That happened on a Friday night or a Saturday night. When I was 16, I used to sneak out on a Friday night and see what sound system was playing. It was best to turn up with a friend because when they open the door they don't recognise you, so somebody usually has to take you in. There was one over near the Tabernacle for years, used to get raided. The police used to do terrible things, smash the sound system and records up or confiscate the drinks. It was illegal. You couldn't get a licence but they were providing a service.

Margaret Stedman (née Riddick):

One of my first memories is the Metropolitan Theatre in Edgware Road. It was turned into a bingo hall later. I must have been 5 years old when my dad first took me. You could stand in the bar and see the stage. He would sit me on an end seat because I couldn't go in the bar. I would be looking at the show and he could still see me while he was having a drink.

Twice a week, my mum would take me to the cinema and sit in the one and ninepennies. I must have been about 4½ when I first went. If my parents went out, I tagged along. One time at the Odeon in Westbourne Grove, they showed *The Ten Commandments* with Cecil B. DeMille doing questions and answers. They were queuing round the block to get in and see that. They used to have talent shows in the Essoldo. They had *Rock Around the Clock* there when that came out and there was trouble when the teddy boys ripped out some of the seats.

Alan Peverall:

My parents used to drink in the Warwick. My dad liked to bet and I used to take his bet and money to give it to a runner, I think he was called Bill. Eventually, they pulled the old streets down and a lot of people moved away, including my friends. Barbara stayed and we had some good times hanging around with other friends, Christine Newman and David, Steven and Linda Cacket, who I eventually married. We used to go to the Wimpy Bar in the Harrow Road, then go to the cinema. We used to have a scam where one would pay to get in then he would go to the toilet and open the fire exit and let the rest in.

Reg Thackeray:

My mum and dad used to go out once a week with my Uncle Dick Miller, who lived at 241 Latimer Road, and his girlfriend. Dick Miller was married but separated from his wife, who lived in Lonsdale Court where Portobello Street used to be. They used to go down the Kenilworth just off Walmer Road.

✒ Roger Rogowski:

Mum and Dad's friends would seem to just come round without any prior arrangement. As we didn't have a phone and we didn't know many people who did, social life just seemed to happen that way. The arrival of two single male friends of my dad's, both Polish, always meant a late night. I don't remember their names except one was young and the other old and, in fact, we only ever referred to him as the Old Man, although not to his face. The routine was always the same. The young man would knock on the door first and give my mum a huge bunch of flowers. This would be followed by the Old Man carrying bags of food and drink, beer and vodka, which would be placed on the dining table in the front room. I was occupied with the gift of a bag of sweets and the occasional pat on the head while the adults ate, drank and talked while the front room filled up with cigarette smoke. At some point in the evening, a music programme would be found on the radio and the Old Man would get up and dance a bit, well a lot really, like Zorba the Greek, stamping on the floor, a point in the evening my parents dreaded as they tried to calm him down to avoid upsetting the Cullens in the flat below, although they were always very good natured about it the next day.

The Old Man was generous to a fault and took me out a few times for a treat. He was a hospital porter. I know he was single and maybe a widower or divorced, and often seemed to act like he had more money than he needed. Whatever his circumstances, he treated me as a kind of part-time son, and once bought me a very smart suit with long trousers, which embarrassed my parents with his generosity.

I'm a bit unsure about my parents' other friends and, anyway, because my dad only had a day off on Sundays and money was tight, they didn't socialise much. They were also friendly with the Cullens in the basement flat and the Littles next door, who used to throw the occasional party. They were boozy and smoky affairs too and, when everyone got a bit tipsy, the adults would end up with some spontaneous singing and dancing including 'Knees up Mother Brown' and the 'Hokey Cokey' with all the appropriate actions. In the days before babysitters, children were just part of the party.

Mossy Condon:

You could tell my dad and my uncle were brothers by looking at them but they sounded different. One day, they went into the Earl of Derby to get a drink. My uncle ordered it and then they heard my dad's accent and the barman said, 'We don't serve your kind in here,' and they had to leave. We all got discriminated against back then. My parents used to go to the Prince Arthur. Everybody had their own favourite place. The Arthur was an Irish pub. They had a few battles where the windows got broken over the years. When we lived in Hazlewood Tower, we would look out the window and always see a fight at closing time. A lot of people don't know but Tom Jones sang in the KPH and the Elgin when he moved here. I think he lived in Colville Square then.

I started going to the Cobden Club for the discos when I was 17, then I played football for the Cobden Club and I played for Grand Union and played for Sutton United, and I played for Hayes for a while. I started at centre half, then I went to midfield and in later years I went to right back. I remember I played for the Cobden Club against the Metropolitan Police in a cup final at QPR in 1971 when we got hammered. We went 2-1 up and lost 7-2.

Barbara Reynolds (née Murray):

My Auntie Alice and Uncle Matey, who lived at 127 Southam Street, had a telly. I was up there every evening with all of them. Every Sunday, the telly would go off and Auntie Alice and all the women used sit and chat, and my Uncle Matey and all the men would go out in the yard and play darts. My family never went to the pub but Gran did go sometimes to the Derby or the Warwick. I was never left on my own as a child and I never had to stand outside the pub. Jet Harris used to visit my gran in Southam House. He called her Auntie Alice and used to go drinking with my cousins in the Derby. His real name was Terry Harris but he was called Jet because he was a fast runner.

Bob Crawley:

Smoking was the big thing for most adults and my parents were no exception, although my mum smoked, I suspect more than most, and it eventually killed her. Dad's pastimes were betting on the horses, never serious money, and having a weekend drink, mostly in the Derby or Warwick. I remember starting to go to the pub on Sunday lunchtimes with my dad, brother, grandfather and uncles. We used to have a £3 or £4 whip-round for drinks, which took a fair amount of weekly pay after Mum had taken her £3 for housekeeping. Dad was also a superb darts player and won many bets and trophies playing the game. Dad was a very easy-going social person and during the war he had known and drunk with John Christie, the Rillington Place murderer.

Although there was no great love for the church, there was an unwritten rule that no one in the family could ever swear while in the company of clergy or while in a church or walking past it, or show disrespect to clergy. Similar rules applied to teachers, nurses and doctors and woe betide anyone in the family who acted differently. A similar approach applied in pubs when women were present, when all swearing was put on hold. Another unwritten rule in the family was that if you took a woman to the pub, be it a girlfriend or family member, they were never permitted to get up and buy a drink. It was always the man's responsibility to take care of everything if you were taking a woman out. An early boyfriend of my sister fell foul of this rule by taking her out but not bringing her home afterwards. He put her on the bus at Neasden and left it at that. She had to walk over the canal bridge in Wedlake Street on her own and this was regarded as terrible neglect.

When the boy next turned up at our door he was told that if he couldn't bring her home, he couldn't take her out, and he was told to clear off. My sister was not best pleased but the boy was never seen again.

Brian Collins:

I was brought up a Catholic so we went to church at St Francis' in Pottery Lane on Sunday. We had our bath on Saturday night. I was an altar server at 11. I had six brothers and sisters and, when we went visiting on Sunday, we would walk from Notting Dale to Harrow Road to catch the bus to Kilburn to see my mum's family and my mum would go over us with a fine-toothed comb to make sure we were clean. We would be in our Sunday best.

I had an Aunt Sally lived in Southam Street and my Auntie Anne lived in Fernhead Road. We always walked from Notting Dale because we didn't have the money for a bus. I liked going to Auntie Anne because my cousins were well-mannered girls. They lived in the same sort of house we had, three floors, and there were three families living in that one dwelling. They were even more tightly crammed in than we were. Their flat was in the basement with two bedrooms on the ground floor where they slept but they had a tiny garden. A garden was what rich people have.

Within ten minutes' walk of our house, there were twenty-three pubs. The Zetland, the Crown and the Portland were my local ones. We started going in pubs when we were 15. There was a culture of underage drinking. You would go in and you would get something like a light ale. Some pubs were more lenient than others. It was probably a bit more controlled, not like now where youngsters drink in parks. You could go in a pub with older family members who would buy the drinks and you could sit in the corner and nurse your light ale. They were great places, although it could turn a little bit violent at times because there were some hard people about. It had that capacity to kick off on Friday or Saturday nights. It was alcohol-fuelled and back then a lot of young men boxed. Sometimes people would come in who weren't local. If you weren't local, you would have to mind your p's and q's and there were some families who had to command respect. If someone was looking at someone else the wrong way all night it could get a bit naughty. The Dale Boxing Club was opposite the Zetland, about 50 yards from where I grew up. My dad was a bit of a boxer when he was younger, so he said to me, 'Why don't you go along?' A lot of young men knew how to look after themselves.

The first youth club I joined was the Rugby Club in Walmer Road. You could join officially at 13 but you could get in at 12. I went to an all boys' secondary school, Cardinal Manning, and so I was going to meet girls at the youth club when I was 13 or 14. It's maybe why I didn't do all my homework because I was so keen to get there in the evening. I would get there virtually when it opened at quarter past seven and stay until about quarter past ten. People came from all over to go there. It was just a fantastic place to go. It was about getting kids off the street and giving them something to do, so you could go along and play table tennis or whatever socialising. People would go along for the music. A lot of people met their future life partners there.

At 18, if you wanted to, you could join the old guard, which was upstairs at the Rugby Club. You had a bar upstairs. As a 14 or 15 year old, we would envy the old guard, who would come in the same entrance and sign in. They had nice clothes and haircuts, they looked fashionable, they looked hard and we were thinking, 'Won't it be great to go up there?' which I did later on. I believe there was the Stowe Club in Paddington funded by Stowe School. My sister didn't want to go to the same youth club as me, so she went to the Harrow Club funded by Harrow School, so there were these very privileged schools who were doing something for the local area.

On Saturday I would get home from David Greig's where I worked, freshen up, get changed and, at 15 and 16, go to a pub or a party. Somebody would always bring a record player and some records. The Duke of Sussex in St Anne's Road was a favourite because there was a young crowd there compared to the Beehive or the Portland. I would finish there then get up at seven in the morning for my paper round.

Susan Mcmahon:

My mum and dad used to go out on Saturday night and they would go to the Tavistock, the Tavi they used to call it, and the Pelican, where they would sometimes go for a drink. When they did that, my older brother had to look after us all.

nine

Work Life

∾ *Frank Hales:*

My dad was a painter and decorator before and after the war but he also had a little business doing up old pushbikes and selling them at the rag fair near the Lancaster Baths. When they painted the outside of houses they had these great big one-piece ladders, which they would wheel about on two barrows. It would take five men to put up and, once it was, it had to stay up all night. They would anchor it at the bottom with sandbags.

Painters' overalls had a big pocket in the front where they put their brushes. One day, my dad was working on a house and the woman asked my dad if he would like some dinner. He said, 'Yes please,' so the woman got him a plate of spaghetti. He'd never seen it before and didn't like it so, when she went out, he stuffed the spaghetti all in his pocket. When the woman came back, she saw the empty plate so she said, 'You must have liked that, would you like any more?' He went out and flushed it down the lavatory.

My mum worked doing the cooking and cleaning for a lady in the posh part of Notting Hill up near Camden Hill. She lived in this big house with wrought-iron railings all the way up to the front door. She was a lovely lady who was shacked up with a famous artist from Poland. She said he was a lodger.

🌸 Ken Farrow:

My first job after I left school in 1960 was as an apprentice butcher in Lockhart's in Harrow Road near the old Coliseum. My father was a dustman working in that area. He knew the people in Lockhart's and he got me a job there. I got fifty bob a week. The first time I had a query, they sacked me. I said, 'They didn't teach me much about butchery at Cardinal Manning.' I also worked at the Feathers in Edenham Street in the evenings after I left school, looking after kids, doing electrical work and helping with the old age pensioners' club. I worked shop hours so, as Thursday was half day closing, I used to do the pensioners' bingo in the afternoons. It was all voluntary work.

I then worked for British Relay for a year, then, in 1963, I volunteered to go in the army but my mum kept writing to my commanding officer to get me out. I then got a job with the council. In the Sixties, you could walk out of one job and into another one. My sister was working for them and

Staff at Dalyte Lighting Company outside the Deco Engineering Works (to the right) in West Row, looking north towards the canal. There were countless businesses of all sizes operating in the area, which meant that local jobs were plentiful. All the buildings in this street have been replaced by flats, although Ruth House in the background still stands today.

she got me a job there when I came out of the army in 1964. I worked in the council depot at the top of Kensal Road for a year. When the depot got too bad, I went into shop work. When I came out the army, I also started working on a salary basis for the Feathers at Dalgarno Way, up the side of the Rootes factory, turn left, near St Francis' Church before the Sutton's. We had a football pitch on the roof and did all our football training up there.

The Feathers had two prefabs in Edenham Street. One was the youth club and one was the nursery during the day and, at night time, it was taken over by the youth club for boxing. There was another building that was a workshop for building boats, which we would take out on the lake in West Drayton. It was there I had the worst day of my life. I was in a new sailing boat we'd just built to try it out. These two boys from the club took out one of the rowing boats, supposed to be unsinkable, and they got to the top end of the lake and turned it over. I was in the sailing boat and someone screamed at me to get over there. I put the sailing boat on the bank and ran over. I swear to this day I saw those two boys running away through the trees but, two hours later, they pulled them out of the lake. To this day, I've never been able to go near the water and I used to love swimming before.

Vic Martin in the 'green shop', 21 Golborne Road, 1960. The shop occupied the site where the wide pavement is now in front of Trellick Tower.

I went from the council depot to work at George Carter's menswear. They had one shop on the Harrow Road, opposite the Prince of Wales cinema, and they had another shop down the road between Bradley and Perrin's and Midland Bank. I worked in both those shops. Then I went to Butler's on the corner of Great Western Road and Fermoy Road. They sold all kinds of household goods. Then I went back to George Carter's, then I went on the buses on the No. 18s and 28s. I got assaulted by some Scottish fans one night coming back from Wembley. They had just won at Wembley. I was standing on the platform at the back, too scared to go upstairs. The bus was swaying from side to side because they were jumping about upstairs. When the bus got back to the garage, I quit straight away.

From there I went to Saxone's selling shoes, then I joined their team setting up new shops. We would spend three or four days sorting out the stock and setting up the displays. We wouldn't go home. We'd just sleep on the carpet in the shop, go out and get something to eat, then go back to work. They had a half dozen of us would go round, pulling us out of our shops. That was about 1966.

✣ Jane Traies:

Taverner's became a bit of a meeting point for people with problems. They used to come and discuss their personal problems with Mum and Dad, almost like the barbers where people used to go and talk about things. Dad opened at six in the morning, when he opened a hatch, not the whole shop. There was a bus stop right outside so people would be going to work, throw their tuppence on the counter and grab the *Herald* or whatever and catch the bus. After nine o'clock, when people had gone to work, he would open the main shop. Dad would have his breakfast and prop open his *Daily Mail* while Mum took a turn in the shop.

When I was at school, I was really rubbish at maths and yet, from 8 or 9 years old, I could give you change for one and elevenpence ha'penny for Players and tuppence for a box of matches out of half a crown without thinking about it. You would count backwards, so if it was eleven pence ha'penny, you would give them a ha'penny and then sixpence to work your way up to half a crown, the coin on the top of the till. Just behind the shop was an office that was stacked up with bars of chocolate and Dad would sit there and cash up every night and we helped him put the coins into piles.

Because we were a sweet shop, right up to 1953 you also had to count the coupons because sweets stayed on ration until then. My dad kept a square tin behind the counter where he put the coupons and they would have to be unfolded and counted every Friday night.

As well as doing newspapers, cigarettes and sweets, my dad took newspaper and magazine orders and, in later years, he'd lay out the papers and in the morning, there would be a Polish daily, the *Weekly Examiner*, the *Herald Tribune*, the *Jamaican Gleaner* and I can remember trying to spell all of the West African names. There was a monthly magazine called *Drum*, which I think was Caribbean. If you looked at all the newspapers and magazines stretched out in the shop, it told you all you needed to know about how the area had changed.

Margaret Burdsey (née Traies):

It was a tobacconists but one of the other things we did was take bookings for a coach company called Ubique. People would come in and say something like, 'I want to go to Blackpool on Saturday,' and I would phone up and say, 'I've got two for the lights in Blackpool,' then I would write out a ticket and hand it over and they would pick up the coach wherever. If our dad was having his breakfast, we would take deliveries like ice cream when it had to go in the fridge quickly. Basically, we helped in the shop from the time we could see over it. I used to help in Grandad's shop in Golborne Road sometimes and occasionally his friend Eric Smith, who used to have a shop over the steps on the corner of Tavistock Road, would ring up and say, 'Can I have some help?' so I used to work over there. Grandad in Golborne Road had a paper round and I would sometimes deliver the papers if his paper boy didn't turn up.

The local nuns from St Charles' Square used to come in. They used to love Mr Traies. He would say to them, 'Is it a fast or a feast?' and, if they said it was feast, he would get a block of ice cream and wrap it in newspaper for them and sometimes they would say it's a fast. When our cat went missing, they all prayed to St Anthony and the cat did come back.

If you're in retail, you're always living six months ahead of everyone else. As soon as Christmas was over, we got the Easter eggs in. We sold a lot of comics, *Dandy*, *Beano*, *School Friend*, and later *Robin*, *Swift*, *Buster*, *Topper*, *Marvel*, *Superman*, *Television Fun*, *Radio Fun*, a huge amount of comics and they each had their Christmas annuals. The annuals would come in in the autumn. We would sometimes go to the warehouse to help choose them. They were lovely with shiny covers. We were avid readers so we said, 'Can we read them?' but Dad said, 'No, they've got to be absolutely new when we sell them.' But we read every annual between October and Christmas but we never opened them more than a few inches so we didn't break the spine.

We got in huge chocolate boxes for Christmas, usually Milk Tray with a picture on and a ribbon. They were just one layer of chocolates and the picture on the front of a kitten in a basket, or a beautiful cottage, or a bunch of flowers. People often kept them and made a picture to hang on the wall out of them afterwards. Dad would display those in the shop window. When people talk about 'that's a real chocolate box cottage', that's where it came from.

They also owned 102 Golborne Road, which was a toyshop. It wasn't open on a regular basis. There was always stock in there and we unlocked it if anyone asked for things. They always ordered more stock for Christmas and Jane, John and I all worked there when we were free, so it was open then. We also opened up to sell fireworks, which we kept in glass cabinets.

John Traies:

We had a corner in the shop called kiddies' corner and I used to sell sweets to my mates basically: lucky dips, lucky bags, flying saucers, shrimps, Spanish Gold. Our mum and dad taught us how to give change. When the customer gave you the money, you put it on top of the till, not in the till, so you could remember what it was, so they couldn't say, 'I gave you two bob there.'

Dad had the most wonderful display of machines outside his shop selling cigarettes, matches, Wrigley's chewing gum, Polos. It was his pride and joy. On a Sunday evening, I used to help fill up the machines with change. Sometimes you would be watching the telly in the evening and there would be this almighty banging on the wall because someone was trying to get his change out of the machine. That was a regular occurrence on a Sunday evening.

I used to serve loose snuff in the Golborne Road shop when I was 12 and measure it out into a paper bag. There was an old girl who used to come in with her nose all eaten away who must have been a snuff addict. I sold the Sunday papers from a stall outside the shop when I got to 15. The main papers were the *News*, *Pic* and *People*, the *News of the World*, *Sunday Pictorial* and *The People*. Posh people would have *The Times* and *The Observer*. We had a Christmas club in both the Ladbroke Grove and the Golborne Road shops. People would come in throughout the year and say, 'Put that half a crown in the Christmas club.' They weren't getting any interest on it, then they would come in later in the year and say, 'How much have I got in the Christmas club?'

Pauline Clark (née Harding):

My father was a chauffeur. The kids in our street thought we were posh because he drove big cars. They thought he was a policeman. He even drove through the war in the pitch dark in the blackouts. Mum sometimes worked in the laundry when they were short-handed.

Dennis Smith:

I left school, had a bit of a holiday and got a job. Then, you could go to work, jack your job in at ten o'clock, walk round the corner and get another job. If there weren't any jobs, there was always a way you could earn a living. I used to go the market to try to get a job on the stalls. One time, someone came to me and said, 'I got some hair dye, go down the 'bella and get a stall.' I got a stall right near the chemist in Golborne Road. I've got a fella walked up and said, 'Have you got any black?' I said, 'I've got a few, how many do you want?' He said he'd buy everything I could get. It was the geezer from the chemist. It was cheaper for him to buy it from us. He bought the lot. I would get a load of gear they put in the police auction. A lot of the stallholders went there.

Alan Warner:

I was coming up to 12 years old. My friend Roger Loveridge and I went to Ladbroke Grove to get onto the cut. We walked up to the Scrubs, where we knew a fair was. I had gone there to see if I could get a summer holiday job. After trying several stalls, I came to one which was a shooting gallery, you know the one where little bottles are placed on a long pole with spiked bits for the bottles to fit on to be shot. I said, 'Any jobs Mister?' and he said, 'Might be son, how old are ya?' 'Nearly twelve,' I said, so he said, 'Can you get here at twelve tomorrow?' I said, 'Yes I can,' and that started a summer holiday I'll never forget.

I got to know some of the fairground lads and thoroughly enjoyed earning a few bob doing something so exciting. The fair finally packed up and the next morning, I was in the Dart Street with Roy Welch playing the machines. Suddenly the door opened and it was John the fairground man I worked for. 'Hello Al. I've just spoken to your Mum and she said you can travel with us to Gosport if you want to,' he said. Now Mum didn't know him from Adam but saying it was OK for her 11½-year-old son to go travelling with a stranger didn't seem likely but I knew that he and his wife Marie were OK, even though she never had much time for this scruffy little fucker from W10. The reason for the offer was that Marie was expecting twins and had little time to help out on the two stalls they owned.

I said 'See ya mate' to Roy and started the adventure. I remember being tucked up in the back of the wagon in the little compartment over the cab. That was my home for the next four weeks. My time off at night was spent with the older lads playing cards or going to the coffee shop in Gosport. It was like having ten big brothers. We all went to a place where there was supposed to be another fairground. On the way one of them popped into a pawn shop to pawn a watch. Like our fairground, the other one was shut on Sunday, too. One night I joined the lads for a game of cards in one of their caravans. We were playing when there was a shout from outside. 'Oi Alan, get out here you thieving little bastard.' I was stunned. I went to get up when one of the lads pushed me back down and said, 'Don't worry Al, I'll sort it.' Of course all the others jumped up too, so I did as well. We got outside and the one that called me out was receiving the hiding of his life. I went to try to pull him off but one of the others just stood in the way. The poor sod was getting nutted all over the place. When we all got back in, the one who did him said to me, 'Al, he thinks you nicked his watch, did ya mate?' I didn't and looked at the lad who shared a van with the one who accused me and he was terrified I was going to say something. That episode apart I had a great time. School had already started when John drove me back. I got home. Mum said 'Hello love' and that was it. I was back to school the next day with some great memories.

I had other jobs as a kid apart from the fairground. One was with a milkman. I would get up early to help him before school and loved it. I was paid half a crown every Saturday morning. It was still horse and cart milkmen in those days. He let me take the reins along Kilburn Lane, remember there was very little traffic in those days. Another was with a rag and bone man called Bob Berry who lived in Lancefield Street. That was also a horse and cart job. Bob one day took me for lunch in the hospital that was along Harrow Road, St Mary's. What food it was, followed by apple pie and custard. Bob was a lovely man, kind and friendly, he took me to the pictures at the Odeon in Kilburn Lane one night with his own kids. Another job was with another totter, Fred Twomey.

Richard Rowlands:

My dad built the Oxford Gardens flats and the flats in Wornington Road next to the school. He was the ganger on that. He was earning a lot of money building all these high-rise flats. My mum was a spotter. She worked for Davis's down Southern Row and then she worked for different dry-cleaners. She would look for marks before they dry-cleaned them and she would get them off. She worked for years. When I used to go to school in Middle Row, she used to get three buses to go to work in Hendon. She left at eight in the morning and never got home until eight thirty at night.

When I left school I was an apprentice bricklayer for a year, then I was a hod carrier, then I was a roofer. Then I was working on the motorway from seven to seven. As soon as I got there, I had to shovel. My wife had a trolley and she went to the Fulham market. I said to her one day, 'How much you took?' and she said, 'A hundred quid,' so I threw the shovel and started in the market because I've got plenty of gab.

Gwen Nelson (née Martin):

Our cat, Bobby, was a regular part of shop life as it was overrun with mice and Dad regularly had to trim the cheese to remove little teeth marks. One day, when he was cutting bacon with one of the old hand-operated machines, a little mouse got trapped by the blade and, before Dad could do anything, he'd chopped off its little back leg. The mouse was dispatched under the heel of Dad's shoe.

Anyone who has watched *Open All Hours* would have a pretty fair idea of what Dad's shop looked like and Dad was like Ronnie Barker in appearance, complete with moustache and full-length coat. The shop had a full front window with the door opening on the left as you faced the shop. Inside were tins of biscuits from which customers chose which they wanted. Tea was sold loose from large wooden chests, usually an ounce or two at a time, and put into a paper bag. He also bought in rice in large chests and one of my after-school jobs was to weigh it into pound bags for sale. A scoop and a quarter weighed a pound and it was amazing how easily one could gauge the amount after a few goes.

At right angles to the window was the counter with a chiller cabinet containing cheeses, salami and bacon. On top of the counter was a set of scales and display stands with packets of Lyons pudding mix, Kraft cheese, Burton's Battenberg cake, and a brand called Kut-a-kake that used to boast that each piece was 'specially wrapped'. On top of the chiller was another glass-fronted display stand with tuppenny caramel wafers, Brand's dressed crab fish paste and butter in 4oz packs, although these were often cut into halves or quarters for customers as rationing was still in force when we moved to North Kensington and, in any case, people could often not afford to buy a whole packet. Behind the counter, he had box shelves made from old packing cases with tinned food in them and plastic strips across them where prices were displayed.

This was before the days of pre-packaging and Dad would cut bacon and ham to order. Bacon was bought by the leg or shoulder from Ivan, Kellets and Child and, one year, Dad negotiated for my school class to have a trip to their smokehouse to see how bacon was made. I can remember the tall chimney with the joints hanging down on hooks, the interior walls of the chimney being stained with a thick, glossy brown substance and the aromatic smoky smell.

Any ends of meat that couldn't be sold, we ended up eating or Mum would mince and add to heaps of potatoes she chopped with onions to go inside the pasties. The pasties were very popular with young working men as they were cheap and tasty. She also made steak and kidney pies and a peculiar mixture of baked beans, tinned peas, corned beef and Oxo cubes, which she would ladle out into dishes the customers brought into the shop. Dad had a very innovative approach and was constantly looking for ways to improve his stock. Up Kensal Road was a wholesalers run by either Czech or Polish people. It was from here Dad bought his salamis and wurst. I often used to walk up there with him and one Christmas, the men gave me a musical box like a carousel that played 'Silent Night'. When West Indian immigrants started to arrive in the late 1950s, they complained that British bread wasn't as good as the bread they got back home, so dad found a West Indian baker who would supply him.

Eggs were bought from a farmer, who would sell them thirty eggs to a tray and also would supply Dad with chickens and geese at Christmas. In those days, chicken was not the ubiquitous food it is today and these birds were delivered feathered and with their interiors still intact. Mum and I sat of an evening after delivery plucking and disembowelling. The trick to plucking is to dampen the feathers first so they don't fly everywhere as you pull them out. Disembowelling was trickier. I was told to be careful of the gallbladder as its rupture would taint the flesh and make the bird unsaleable. Most of these birds were old layers and often one would find an egg inside them or a string of yolks before the shell had formed around them.

Although Dad had a till, he refused to add up purchases on it as he could do it in his head quicker and often more accurately than punching the keys and pulling the handle. If a customer demurred, he'd let them add up on the machine while he did it in his head and he always finished first and was correct. Cigarettes were a large part of his sales. Packs of twenty were available, but more often, people bought packs of ten or even two. Popular brands were Kensitas for the coupons you collected and could exchange for gifts, Senior Service, Dunhill, Craven A, Players and a brand especially for the ladies, Sweet Afton. A very upmarket brand was Sobranie. You could buy strong-smelling Black Russian or a milder one, Cocktail, with the cigarettes each a different pastel colour. Like butter, cigarette packets were also split and one cigarette would be bought at a time if the person didn't roll their own. Tinned tobacco and cigarette papers were more common, as very thin fags could be rolled and men would spend all day with a partially smoked dog-end attached to their lower lip.

Customers were a mixed bunch. Many were very poor and had a real struggle to make ends meet. While Dad was far from a soft touch, he was aware of genuine hardship, having had to leave home at 12 years old and become self-supporting because of his father's remarriage. He would allow people things on tick until their situation improved and often gave away slightly smelly bacon or sausages that were past their best. Some of the best customers Dad had were the Irish navvies who had come over after the war to work on the roads. These were young, well paid and hungry as a result of their hard labour. They would buy bacon by the pound, eggs by the dozen and a whole loaf of bread and 4oz of butter, and that just for one meal. At the other end of the scale were women with children and no man to support them. Illegitimacy rates were high around North Kensington and I suspect a lot of women were on the game to support their children. All too often, this resulted in another mouth to feed unless a trip to the local back street abortionist could be afforded. Rumour had it that one operated from one of the basements in Edenham Street using a pint of gin and a knitting needle to perform the task. Dad could always be relied on to find a little something for a woman who was trying to raise her children decently despite her circumstances.

Before people had telephones, the traveller was a regular weekly visitor to dad's shop. These men were employed by warehouses to visit shops and persuade them to buy their goods. They were paid on commission, so were persuasive salesmen. Dad got on well with them and was always keen to get a bargain and pass it on to his customers, so would negotiate a special weekly deal on a particular line.

Although my parents gave me a very generous 10s a week pocket money while I was at grammar school, as I grew older I wanted to buy records, make-up and trendy clothing to compete with other girls, so I got an after-school job two days a week at Bowen, the chemist's along the road from Mum and Dad's shops. My work was out the back filling bottles with various potions and tonics that were in gallon jars. There was a brilliant orange, sticky iron tonic; a red, equally sticky vitamin tonic and a pink, vaguely minty-smelling indigestion mixture. I had a large funnel with which to decant the mixture into the bottles but the weight of the gallon jar usually meant I was unable to lift it upright in time to stop the smaller bottle overflowing, resulting in a mess that was very difficult to clean up or hide from Mr Bowen. Too much spillage meant my wages were adjusted to compensate for the loss. There were also labels to stick on the bottles that had to be processed through a roller that sat in a container of water and dampened the glue on the back of the labels. The roll of labels had to be fed through the roller at a certain speed to make the glue adhesive without causing the paper to disintegrate. I was better at this than filling the bottles but less accurate when it came to sticking the labels on the bottles and they tended to have a drunken appearance instead of being in alignment.

As well as medication, Bowen's sold a large variety of other items, including trusses and gentlemen's requirements. One of my abiding memories is when one of the local toms came in and asked for 'Frenchies'. Mr Bowen handed her a packet of Durex, only to be told in a very loud voice that she 'didn't want them effin' rubber things' but she wanted the ones you could wash out and hang on the line.

As well as working in Bowen's, I had a Saturday job in one of the shoe shops up the lane. Very few shoes were on display and it was up to customers to say what they were looking for and for the staff to locate it out the back of the shop while the person was seated on one of the benches that ran the length of the inside of the shop. There was a method to this as much of the stock was from previous years and, if you could shift any old stock, you'd get a bonus for the sale. It was expected that the saleswoman would squat on a stool at the customer's feet and put the shoes on for them to try. By and large people kept themselves clean but some fairly hummed when they took off their shoes. One man had dreadful feet with thickened, yellow nails that curved over his toes and grew back underneath them. How he managed to walk I don't know. Other feet were equally disgusting with toe jam and areas of hardened skin. I only worked here a short time. One Saturday I arrived at my usual starting time to be told by the manager that my services were no longer required and I could turn round and go home as he'd found a replacement for me. I had been given no warning or told that I needed to improve my work, so I was very upset. When I told Dad what had happened he asked if I'd been paid in lieu of notice and received holiday pay. On learning that I hadn't, he went down with me and threatened the manager with all sorts of legal action if he didn't pay up. The manager caved in and gave me the money.

Charlie Phillips:

There was only about three firms where everybody used to go to. Cadby Hall in Hammersmith was owned by Joe Lyons. They were a big employer of black people. The Metal Box Company in Park Royal. My dad worked at the Metal Box Company. Some people worked in the Lucozade factory in Great West Road. Others, if they're not nurses or orderlies, would work on

London Transport or British Railways. The main employer was Joe Lyons. They had coffee houses all over the place. When you went to St Charles' and Queen Mary's Hospitals, most of the nurses were from Ireland and the Caribbean. One of the biggest disappointing things is that they've taken some of our most talented people and they had to come here and do menial jobs but a lot of them were well-qualified people.

When I was 13 I got my first paper round. I used to deliver newspapers in Southam Street. I used to work for A.J. Murray. He used to have a newsagent's in Portobello Road. I joined the Merchant Navy in 1963 and sailed around the world. When I came back from sea, I used to stay with my parents.

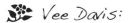 Vee Davis:

I got my first job at Osram the very week I arrived. I didn't hang about. I got up in the morning. It dark like hell, I'm thinking when will I see the sun because you go to bed, it dark, you get up in the morning, it dark because it was November and those days they had that smog and fog and everything looked black. Even the clothes that people wear look black. Everybody was in grey and black, no colours, no nothing. So I got up that morning. Someone had told me how to get to register. It used to be they had that DHSS on Westbourne Park where the 28 bus go. Osram used to be right where Tesco's is now in Brook Green. The whole big building was Osram. When I got there, they didn't tell me what I'm making. I was sitting there doing something with anodes and cathodes, looking down a sort of microscope and you see these little things and you have to straighten them. Somebody said it was for the war. I don't know what the hell I was doing but I was doing it. I think it was £5 something a week I used to get, but that was plenty money. I paid me rent with that, we had food to eat and I could still get a nice top to go and party that weekend.

I didn't understand the English too good. They used to call me Taffy, a bloody Welsh woman, because of my singsong voice. I was the first blackie who worked in the anode and cathode section. They were giving me hell, calling me Golliwog. When they was going Blackie and Sambo and all of this, I wonder what the hell they were talking about because to me, the English people were speaking fast, faster than me. I was too busy thinking how much money I was going to send to my parents in Trinidad. My supervisor,

Redmond, she was fantastic woman, English woman. She always coming behind the screen and cuddle me and say things like, 'Don't take no notice of them.' And I said, 'What the hell you talking about? Take no notice of what?' They just couldn't get along with me because it was like they didn't want a black woman in there, a black person, let alone a woman but I never used to worry, I just do the job and what I have to do.

I think I stayed there about four or five years, because after there, I worked for this Jewish man on Shepherd's Bush, scything leather. You remember those shoes they used to make, like plaited shoes but they were all done on a machine, like different bits of leather. They called it scything, where they pass the leather through to get that smooth effect. I stayed there for about a year and a half, I didn't stay long. I think that was £5 or £6 a week.

I was getting ready to go back home. It was like I came here for a certain time and it's time for me to go back. It had a lot of complications, like missing home. So after five and a half years I did go back home. It was a different picture. It wasn't what I thought, everything had changed. I used to think I was Cinderella, so everything would work out nice, I'd get married and have some children. It didn't happen. When I came back, I went and worked with this same people again. They write to me while I was in Trinidad saying, 'Isn't your holiday over? Why don't you come back?' Then I came back and went right to them to work again. It was a small place. About ten or twelve worked there.

Then I did my nursing. I start it in Fulham Hospital. The space is now taken up by Charing Cross Hospital. By the time I finished, I qualified, I went over to work in Charing Cross. I was just general nursing. I say it myself but I think I was the best nurse they could ever have. Well, the patients used to tell me that, as soon as you come the sun shine. They were fantastic, I was so lucky that I met nice people and I worked hard. The patients were lovely. To me all nursing was about looking after your patient.

It was so much hard work but in those days, I used to work for the agency all night to make my extra money. In my time it was a place in Praed Street, opposite St Mary's. I just had to pick up that phone and boom, to St Charles' tonight and you go to so and so tonight, and then you get the money in hand. Cash-in-hand used to be good, so I never used to think much of me monthly money, remember that going in the bank from the hospital. I'm permanent at that hospital but I do agency work. I loved me job but doing the agency was a cover, so I wouldn't complain about me wages when it comes through the bank, I get extra in hand. It meant me husband would look after the children in the night. I did nights for five years, straight nights. I come back in the morning, my husband leave, I look after the children. It was mad. I had the last boy and to take him to the nursery at one o'clock and he used to get so impatient, and he would come and wake me and go, 'Mum, you're going to be late.' You wouldn't hear the clock, I get up and say, 'Can't you let me sleep a little more?'

✤ Margaret Stedman (née Riddick):

My dad worked at the LWD, the London Wholesale Dairy in Scrubs Lane that turned into United Dairies later on. They used to punch the bottle tops, four different colours, out of long strips of foil on a machine. He would bring home the strips left over with the holes in and sold them to all the local pubs, including the Brit, and they would hang it up as their decorations at Christmas. Before he worked at the dairy, he was a driver and before that he worked on the Great Western Railway.

My first job was at Marks & Spencer's in Hammersmith, then my mum, who worked in White Knight, got me a job working in the laundry. I later worked for Sunlight.

✤ Ray Matthews:

My dad worked as a bus conductor when I was young. My mum, Louisa, had two cleaning jobs and did homework making linings for fur coats. We also went to a factory in Walmer Road to collect fibreglass fishing rods that were coated in plastic. We had to remove the coating and make the rods clean. We got paid a ha'penny for each rod and it could take up to half an hour to do each one. We loved it if one would strip in about a minute. Not often that happened. I also used to hire a handcart when I was about 10 or 11 and go totting newspapers. Wet a couple of papers in the middle and it weighed more. With lead pipe, put a bit of dirt in the middle and tap the ends over and it weighed more. They always paid by weight. I also collected rags and woollens, and woollens were worth more.

 *Babs Coker:*

My mum worked in Barlby Road School and she had a cleaning job at night. My dad was head porter at St Charles' Hospital. I remember going to a lady's house whose daughter took me to school because my mum worked.

Alan Peverall:

I had lots of jobs in the area, Fidelity Radio, Roseblades the tinners in Bramley Road, Hytec, Pilgrim Payne, Saxby in Latimer Road, Chinacraft, Oliver Toms in Kensal Road and on the buses. Most of them were boring and just a way of earning a wage.

Reg Thackeray:

My dad was a haulage contractor. He cleared rubbish, cleared houses, taking stuff round to the builder and what have you. In the beginning, my mum worked on the Great Western Railway, which she loved, loading and unloading trucks. When my dad got busy later, he made her pack up work to be at home as a housewife and answering the telephone for his business. Along the road from the Kenilworth was a row of three-storey houses. My dad knew the man who owned them and rented them out. He offered my dad the whole row for nothing. They needed a lot doing to them including bathrooms putting in so my dad didn't want to know.

My sister, when she left school in the 1940s, worked in Woolworths on the Portobello Road on the sweet counter. The manager in there had a club foot and kept picking on my sister. One day, my mum went down there and sorted him out. He was as nice as pie to her after that. At the age of 12, before I left school, I started working down the market with a laundry basket on wheels selling bits and pieces from my dad that he'd got on jobs. Later on, I took a stall in my sister's name because I wasn't old enough and, after that, there was another fella I helped out on a Saturday and got two quid for. He always gave me change, never notes.

You just turned up. Price's used to put up all the tables all the way along Golborne Road. You came along and, if it wasn't someone's regular pitch, you would put your stuff on the stall and the market inspector would come round with a book and you paid him and you had your licence for the day. A lot of people would just leave what they didn't sell at the end of the day and you'd get their stuff and sell that too and make a few bob. A lot of the neighbours would give me bits and pieces as well. One time, my dad did a job in a lab in Harley Street collecting bottles with people's organs in. There was a skeleton all wired up in a wooden box. In the morning I went down the market with the skeleton and sold it for £60. That was a fortune. One job in Harley Street, there was a rolled up canvas painting which I had framed and sold.

I also went with my dad doing jobs and I got to know the fella who owned Harper's toy and record shop and helped him out. I loved it. I used to be there until two o'clock in the morning sometimes doing the window displays, it was so enjoyable. The local bobby used to come by checking the door handles and got to know me. When I was helping out in the toyshop, Mr Siegal at No. 93, which also used to be Harper's, got fed up so he was let out of the lease and we started an arcade there because it's 60 foot from front to back, so we were able to get in sixteen stalls and a coffee bar. I used to go in and collect the rent for the man who was in charge of it. When he decided he wanted to pack up and go to Spain, I got to take it over completely and I used to rent out the flats upstairs and Harper's and that was all £16 a week. In 1977, I had the opportunity to buy Clarke's. I was very friendly with the lady who owned it. I looked after her cats when she went to the Isle of Man to play golf. The place was in a terrible state. The floorboards had worn away where people had walked over the years. I carried on selling pet foods until eight years ago, when it wasn't really worth it any more. The shopfront was fitted in 1869 by Thomas Ireland, who built the place, and it's unchanged. The pine shutters are original from about 1870 and cost £4 10s back then.

Marg Pithers:

My grandad got my dad his job through his connections at the Harrow Boys' Club. My dad said he wanted to be a carpenter but my nan said, 'No, you're going to be a barrister's clerk.' It was a very good job although it was a lot of pressure. In those days you got a tenth of the barrister's earnings because it was the clerk's job to go out touting for work. My dad was paid commission quarterly and he would treat us when he got paid. Other times he was just on basic. Later, he did the court circuit so he was away a lot during the week.

My mum worked in the Home and Colonial Stores in Portobello Road. Old people would come in at Christmas, very poor, and ask for just two slices of chicken or two slices of beef and they would put extra in the bag for them and put a penny or more on the bills of people who looked like they could afford it. My mum later worked in Dorothy Perkins in High Street Ken at one time and she used to say, 'They might think they're posh there but their underwear is disgusting.'

I got a Saturday job quite young at Holm's the bakers in Golborne Road. They did the best doughnuts in the world. Saturday mornings, it was heaving. People would queue out the door for their bread. When I first worked there, all I did was keep the shelves full with bread and rolls and cakes. Mrs Meyer had a stern exterior but she would say, 'Eat as many cakes as you want but don't eat them in the shop. Go out the back and eat them.' After three weeks you wouldn't want to touch another cake. When you finished work, she would pay you, which wasn't a lot, about a quid but then she'd give you two massive loaves, a bag of rolls, a big bag of at least a dozen doughnuts and two big fresh cream cakes. You could barely carry it all. When I got home, they would all be waiting for me. I worked all day Saturday and I would go in school holidays as well.

They had another shop further down Golborne Road where they baked and iced the cakes. Mrs Meyer's brother was a master baker. One day, they made a wedding cake about the size of a table with a bouquet of roses on the top and trellis icing all the way round. Somebody rushed out with a tray of sausage rolls and smacked it into the side of the cake. The bride walked in and went into hysterics, shouting and crying. The brother told her not to worry and he took the cake into the back and built it up and re-iced it. On Friday, Mrs Meyer would stay there all night while they baked the bread in the basement. It must have been like Hades down there with the heat. They would all have their breakfast there and, at eleven o'clock, she would make a big pot of coffee you could have stood a spoon in and a big plate of jam doughnuts. At the back of the shop they had a gas fridge, upstairs was the bedroom that Mrs Meyer would sleep in on Friday nights and on the top floor, they stored all the paper you would wrap bread in and boxes for the cakes.

✍ Roger Rogowski:

My dad's education was interrupted by the war and he must have spoken very little English when he arrived in the UK in 1946, so he took any job he could after he was demobbed in 1947. He went to work in a bakery, although I don't know where that was. In 1957, after my dad's English must have improved, he got a job in the accounts department at Limmer and Trinidad Asphalt Company in Carnwath Road in Fulham but he also continued to work at the bakery on Friday nights and Saturday afternoons. It meant he was a bit of a shadowy figure at times and it's no exaggeration to say he probably hated doing a second job. After his Saturday shift at the bakery, he always brought home a couple of loaves of bread and cakes, such as apple turnovers and jam doughnuts, and he would always try to make up for his absence by taking us out on Sunday to a park for a kickabout or to see the sights in central London. My mum was a cinema usherette until I came along and they moved to Westbourne Park. My dad had quite a conservative attitude about women working, so he would rather half kill himself doing two jobs rather than ask my mum to be anything than a full-time housewife.

👁 Mossy Condon:

When my dad came over, he was a carpenter and he worked in Kensal Road in a joiner's shop called Griffith's opposite the Britannia. He didn't have far to walk. He could walk to work in three minutes. My dad was working nearly every day of the week. He used to start early and come home at seven at night. When he did have a day off, when there wasn't any exhibitions on, he'd do some work indoors like make little coffee tables and little bedside cabinets and sell them for £2 each, which was quite a lot of money. He'd do that to make up extra money. He would sell them just to other people in the street. They would be veneered mahogany.

My dad left Griffith's and went to Westend Lane to work for Beck and Pollitzer's. My mum worked on the No. 7 bus as a clippie and then she went to Securicor driving the small vans. My mum had shift work because she was on the buses, so she would have some days off and when she went to Securicor she only worked Monday to Friday, so she had Saturday and Sunday off.

When I got a bit older I worked down Golborne Road for Geoff, who used to sell ladies' tights and socks, and I worked for him for about a year. Then I worked for Sheila King, who had a fruit and veg stall outside Hopwood's the butcher's, then I done a paper round. I used to deliver the *Evening Standard* and the *Evening News* and the Sunday papers and then I would do the morning papers at 7 o'clock before I went to school, round Wornington Road, St Ervans Road and Golborne Gardens. Then I worked for an ice-cream parlour making lollies. You had to work because the money wasn't around and children didn't get much pocket money.

🐚 Barbara Reynolds (née Murray):

I used to work for Sipp's the hairdresser's Monday, Wednesday, Friday and Saturday washing and drying hair and I got twenty-five bob a week plus tips. I started at the hairdresser's when I was 13. That was my evening job after school. Then I started a job in Woolworths down Portobello Road on a Saturday. I was on broken biscuits and cakes. Then I worked at Ravel's in Kensington High Street.

🐚 Bob Crawley:

Dad worked in heavy industry in Acton and Mum was a chambermaid in a hotel in South Kensington. A tip from a hotel guest was a big issue for Mum so, when I stay in a hotel, I always leave something for the cleaning staff.

I first started work in a shoe shop under Hazlewood Tower to earn the money to go on a trip abroad with the Scouts. My mum and dad couldn't afford it because it was thirty quid to go. Tom Vacca, Chris Clifton and me all worked in the shoe shop covering different areas. I would knock on every door in Octavia House and ask if they had any shoes that needed repairing. Another week, I would do Adair and Hazlewood Towers and Bosworth House. Soles and heels were seventeen and six and people would give you a quid and say keep the change.

I did that for a couple of years until I went to secondary school, then I worked for Sado and King's the off-licence in Harrow Road near Amberley Road. Our big seller was Newcastle Brown Ale and the winos would come in for cheap Cyprus sherry to knock them out quick. I would bring up the crates from the cellar to the shop and deliver to customers for £1 14s a week. There was an old girl by Royal Oak station who would put a big order in for Amontillado sherry and wine every week and I would put the crate on the front of my bike and cycle it down to Royal Oak and take it up in the lift. I was only about 14 at the time, so I shouldn't have been working in the off-licence at all.

Christine Smith:

We didn't have a washing machine for many years but the Sixties saw launderettes arrive and my first job, aged 9, was to use the large spinner to help clients spin their clothes before putting them in a drier. The spinner cost one old penny. I got sixpence for the whole Saturday. I used to take my mum's washing to the launderette and get it washed, spun and dried and then get on with my job.

Brian Collins:

My dad would cycle from home to wherever the job was. He would come in from work and have his body wash while Mum made his tea. He would say, 'I've been to Ilford,' or 'I've been to Islington.' He would dig ditches in all weathers and cycle home. To supplement my dad's income, my mum worked in Addison Avenue cleaning for a well-to-do family. In later years, when I was in my teens and we were all a little bit more independent, my mum would get the train from Holland Park station to the city and do cleaning for the banks in the evening and get home in the early hours and see us up in the morning to go to school.

I wouldn't call it a job but I never had enough money so me and my friend Michael, who lived just along from me in Princedale Road, at 10 or 11 years old, would nick a bucket and sponge from my mum and go car cleaning. In our streets, there were very few cars, so we would go round the corner to Addison Avenue, Lonsdale Crescent or Lonsdale Road, where the really big posh houses were. We would just knock on doors and say, 'Can I clean your car?' Sometimes they would say OK and sometimes they wouldn't like the look of us or trust us to do it. We cleaned a few exotic cars. I remember cleaning an Alfa Romeo and I'd never heard of an Alfa Romeo. My mate and I would clean the car and say, 'Do you want us to clean the inside for a little bit more?' and we'd get a dustpan and brush from somewhere. We would clean cars for pence and spend them on the way home, sometimes in the baker's at Clarendon Cross.

I struck lucky at 12 when I got a job delivering papers for Eric's the newsagent's up at Clarendon Cross. I was the rookie so they gave me the longest route and then I started delivering in the posh streets towards Holland Park Avenue. I got paid a pound a week for that. They would have papers like *The Times* with all the supplements on Sundays so Eric said, 'Do you have a pushchair to carry all those newspapers?' We would all meet up about twelve o'clock at the top of Lonsdale Crescent after we'd finished and get on our pushchairs and bomb downhill down the Clarendon Road, hoping there weren't any cars at the bottom.

As a 14-year-old, I got a job in David Greig's in Portobello Road opposite the bug'ole. I worked there until I was nearly 17 on Saturdays and in school holidays serving behind the counter. It was a thrill to see who would come in the shop and serve them. Richard Neville, who founded *Oz* magazine, was a regular in that shop buying his cheese and bacon, just doing ordinary stuff. I would always try to serve Mr Neville. We had all sorts of celebs in. I still needed more money so I would finish there at six o'clock, have a bit of a break and then help some of the stallholders clear away some of the barrows or sweep up because they wanted to get to the pub to have a pint or count up their money.

⚘ Susan Mcmahon:

My mum used to do cleaning in offices in the West End. She had about five or six jobs. She would go out at four thirty in the morning and her job would start about five thirty, then she would get back about eight to get us ready for school. She done it for years. My dad was a crane driver on the building sites and then he started working in an office as a premises manager.

ten

Holidays

❧ Frank Hale:

When I was at St Francis' School, the church organised a trip to Dymchurch. We camped out for a week in the grounds of a big church. They gave us mattresses we had to fill with straw and we were encouraged to write letters home.

🌡 Ken Farrow:

There was the Country Holidays Fund, which meant you could go away and stay with a family and go year after year. I went to a family in Guildford arranged through the school. One of my sisters stayed with a family in Dorking. The parents would take us out, play games in the garden and treat us like one of their kids.

🌸 Jean Russell (née Hemming):

In the summer my dad used to go fishing in Iver for a weekend with the other men in the street. The farmer who owned the field in Iver said to my dad, 'You can use the field and camp as long as you keep the field clean and tidy but I let the cows in the field in the morning.' Half the street would go to Iver camping. We had a great big bell tent because there was a lot of us. My cousins had a smaller tent. There was all different tents in a group. We

Ladies' day trip to Margate, outside the Portobello Star, July 1952. The Portobello Star is now a cocktail bar of the same name.

On the way to St Andrew's School holiday on the Isle of Wight, teachers and children pose for a photograph on HMS *Victory*, 1955.

cooked on an open fire. Someone found a freshwater spring in the next field. My mum cooked a big roast dinner on that open fire.

We would sit round the fire and sing songs at night. We would just sleep on the floor, no beds. Going, all the men used to have tents on their backs and their fishing rods. My mum would load up a pram with pots and pans and bedding and we walked all through the streets to Westbourne Park station, put it in the guard's van and that's how we got to Iver. My Auntie Hazel, she was like a caricature, a fat lady with a big bust and tiny size three feet. Anyway, one day all the cows were coming in the field and she crawled out of the tent with nothing on the top and she called out to my dad, 'Here you are Ted. I'm all ready for milking.' All the aunties collapsed laughing. That's what they were all like, they were hilarious. That was our only holiday. We would walk all through the woods exploring. My cousin was a tomboy. She would dip a stick in cow poo, put it on our foreheads and we were her slaves for the day. We had to walk around all day with this cow poo on our foreheads.

✿ Jane Traies:

We went once or twice to Rottingdean with the Girl Guides. We stayed in a convent. There was a connection with the church in Ladbroke Grove. There were a lot of fallen women there running the laundry. Going from Ladbroke Grove to the beach at Rottingdean and seeing Birling Gap was lovely. The garden in the convent was lovely. They had their own cow and had their own milk. They kept a pig. We had to go to their services. We gave a little show for the nuns. We were in separate rooms with iron bedsteads and just brick walls. It was very spartan with bare floorboards and newspaper in the toilets and the food was ghastly but we loved it.

ℰ John Traies:

We went to Broadstairs with our granny for holidays. Later, we took a cottage in Newick, which was very rural. Latterly we had a caravan near Worthing and Dad would come down and join us after shutting the shop on Saturday night and drive down. We went to France in 1966 on our first foreign holiday when we drove over with the caravan and I saw the World Cup Final in France surrounded by Germans.

Maureen Rafferty (née Coker):

I remember going on school holidays to the Isle of Wight twice for two weeks. The trip was organised by St Andrew's school. Mr Brackley, one of the teachers, organised the trips and came along. We stayed at 14 St George's Road in Shanklin.

Alan Warner:

I had many cousins in the street but also some good friends. One of them was Roger Loveridge, who was like another cousin. His family and nearly all the aunts and uncles went for a two-week camping holiday every summer to Iver in Buckinghamshire. One of our fathers knew the farmer in the area and he allowed us exclusive use of a field that ran alongside the River Ouse. The biggest part of the camping holiday was the long walk to Westbourne Park station. It seemed to always be a bright sunlit morning when we set out at around eight o'clock. The walk was magical as we had the whole holiday in front of us. At that time trains were steam-powered and had single-compartment carriages. All us kids would get into one carriage and at every stop to Iver, we would all crowd around the door to stop anyone else getting into our compartment.

There was a cattle crossing where we camped and it was usual to get out of the tent in the morning and step barefoot into a cowpat. I have lovely memories of those times, playing cricket or football, climbing the highest trees and carving my name on the bark. At night, we would sit around a campfire just having a laugh and, once we settled down, we would hear the parents coming back from the pub singing. I remember one Saturday morning, twinnies Len and Dave would take us kids to Saturday morning pictures via the canal path. We had just got going when Dave said, 'Everyone lay on the floor.' There was a man pointing a shotgun in our direction. We all panicked and did as we were told. The twins were in a heated conversation with the man but it turned out the gun wasn't loaded and it just happened to be pointing our way. We used to go to another part of the canal for fishing and on the bank was a hut lived in by a family of three, I never knew the make-up of the family as they were all adults but the hut was very smelly, as were the family. I remember their names were Punch, Lardy and Fred.

One night, my elder brother and I had been into Iver with our parents and sat outside the Fox and Pheasant. On the way there, we had to go across what used to be a bridge over the Ouse but there was just a girder to walk across. In daylight it was easy but coming back in the dark, Dad insisted we be carried across on someone's shoulders. Fred was one option. The other was Dad. Neither of us wanted to sit on Fred's shoulders, so Dad tossed a coin. I lost and was terrified Fred would drop me in the river but we all landed safely on the other side.

My Uncle Tig Hough was always with us. He and the other adults had many friends in Iver and, one day, one of the families had a little boy missing and they asked for help looking for him. Sadly it was Uncle Tig who found the poor mite dead in the river. Uncle Tig was a big gentle man but not long after he was diagnosed with cancer and died some time later. Everyone said it was him finding the child that had caused his cancer.

🌿 Richard Rowlands:

We used to go to Southend and go and queue up at Holms in the morning and get twenty-four rolls and mum would make up twenty-four rolls and we would get on the train and we would be down Southend all day. It was like paradise.

🌿 Gwen Nelson (née Martin):

Back in the 1950s and '60s there was no such thing as shutting a shop to go away on holiday, so it was usually Mum and I who went away for a week to the seaside or a country town while Dad manned the shop on his own. Obtaining somewhere to stay involved writing away to advertisements in newspapers and much back and forth of letters before dates were settled and accommodation booked. Very few people went abroad for their holidays. When I first started grammar school, I was very envious of one of the other girls whose stepfather was the director of a theatre. Every year they spent the entire summer holiday in a villa in the South of France.

We always stayed in bed and breakfast establishments. I don't think the idea of a hotel ever crossed my mum's mind. They were for posh people, not working class. Bed and breakfast was exactly what it said. Rooms were single, twin or double with shared facilities, on the same floor as your room if you were lucky, but mostly up or down a couple of flights of stairs. Breakfast was usually sausage, egg and bacon with cereal and toast that would set you up until teatime. You were expected to leave the house straight after breakfast and stay out all day until about four o'clock, no matter what the weather. On one occasion we had gone away to Margate not long after Mum had had a tooth pulled by a brutal dentist who had fractured her jawbone and, as a result, she developed an abscess. The weather was foul and we spent most of the holiday in Dreamland or one of the many seafront cafes. Mum was dosing herself on aspirin and wearing a plastic raincoat over her woollen cardigan. She emanated a peculiar smell but I could never work out if it was the medication, the purulence or the combination of plastic and wet wool.

When I was about 8 or 9, the nuns at St Mary's suggested to my parents that they send me for a week to one of their sister convents. I can't remember exactly where it was, maybe Bexhill or Broadstairs. Mum took me there and left me to the care of the nuns. As soon as she had gone my suitcase was taken off me and my clothes put on a shelf in a locked cupboard. I was to sleep in a dormitory with a lot of other girls. The food was dreadful. Porridge was the only breakfast option, without sugar. Lunch was typical school dinners and you weren't allowed to leave the table until your plate was cleared of all fat and congealed gravy. Tea was bread and jam and fruit squash. During the day we had various activities and games to pass the time but the nights were awful with strange noises and listening to at least one of the other girls snoring. It was the first time I had been away from my parents and I was frightened and homesick. I cried during the night but, instead of sympathy and understanding from the nuns, I was transferred to another dormitory where there were babies and very young children because they said that would teach me not to be a cry baby. I managed to catch a cold while I was there too but was only allowed one handkerchief a day, even though mum had packed plenty, so I had to use my cuff or the front of my vest when the nuns weren't looking. I was glad to see Mum when my week was up.

In 1962, the year I left school, Mum and I were invited up to Scotland for a holiday. When Mum was a child, she had a South African pen friend. Margaret had trained as a nurse and, during the war, met a Scottish soldier, Scotty. Dad was unable to spare the time away from his shop, so I was also invited. It was a big adventure involving an overnight rail journey to Dundee. Scotty was there to meet us with his car. This, again, was an adventure as we didn't know anyone who owned their own car. We were ushered into the lounge where their elder son, Derek, was with Keith his best friend from school. As we went in, Keith looked up and our eyes met. It is not too much of an exaggeration to say I heard the sound of violins and felt my heart race. For the whole time I was up there we were inseparable, except for when he went home at night. At the end of the holiday we exchanged addresses and phone numbers.

 Jeannie Rowe (née Searson):

We had a simple life, no car and no television. For holidays we went to stay with our grandparents in Glasgow. They had a garden and kept hens, so we experienced a different kind of life. My grandfather took me out and about in Glasgow telling me about the history and the famous sights. Nearly all our relatives lived in Scotland. We used to go by coach overnight.

Charlie Phillips:

I didn't know what a holiday was but we used to have a lot of outings. The first outing I went to was on Jamaican Independence Day in 1962. My dad rented a sound system and drove all the way up to Wolverhampton and played in a big military hall. Barry Island was a very popular place, and Margate, too. People would rent a hall and get together. We made our own entertainment.

Ray Matthews:

We were lucky to have my mum's parents, who were such lovely people. My nan always arranged outings for every bank holiday down to Brighton, Southsea or Hastings. They were beautiful days that we wanted to last forever. Although we were very poor, we always had a holiday when I was young. It was hop picking on a farm near Leeds Castle in Kent and, when we were slightly older, it was St Mary's Bay. My dad had a bad drink problem. I can't criticise him as I don't know what he saw during the war while he was in the Navy, but he never drank while we were on holiday, which made it so magical.

🦋 *Babs Coker:*

We never went on holiday but used to go to Southend for the day. My parents couldn't afford an actual holiday, just days out. I was sent to Broadstairs with the Children's Country Holidays Fund once. I think it was to get kids out of London into the cleaner air in the country.

🐝 *Alan Peverall:*

Like most people in the area, my parents didn't have a lot of money, so we never had a holiday until I was about 15, when we had a week in Newhaven.

🍄 *Reg Thackeray:*

I've never been on holiday ever.

🐞 *Marg Pithers:*

When we got our first car, we drove to Westgate and we were stuck on a caravan site for the whole week. When my mum's aunt died, we went to a caravan in Cornwall. We saw peacocks for the first time and ran back screaming because we'd never seen them before.

🐌 *Roger Rogowski:*

We never went away for a holiday, although my mum, me and later Chris were always packed off for about four weeks during the school summer holiday to stay with my grandad, who had been a widower since 1958 and lived on his own in Northfields. He had a garden and, better still, there were large parks nearby. The woodland by the canal close by was a place of adventure and, although it was the same Grand Union Canal, it was different from the canal at the back of Kensal Road. The roads were lined with trees and all of the front gardens were filled with shrubs and flowers. It was like an alien environment where it was more common to see bees, spiders, butterflies and beetles than the flies of Kensal Road. It seems mad now looking back on it because it was only about 6 miles away. I got into trouble one day though, when I found my nan's fox fur stole in her wardrobe, tied a length of string round its neck, and took it for a walk along the street. I don't think I was ever found out borrowing my mum's can of hairspray, which made a great flamethrower for incinerating ants and woodlice in the garden.

I was 6 when I first saw the sea and I remember being slightly startled that it actually made a noise when it hit the beach. My uncle and aunt picked us up from Kensal Road in their two-tone green Hillman Minx and drove us to West Wittering through various small towns and villages. In one small village, I saw a crocodile of schoolchildren holding hands walking along the road and wondered what it must be like to go to school in such a strange place.

Mossy Condon:

With a lot of the Irish families, the children would be sent over to Ireland for five weeks and they would bring them back just before the new term started. I had a friend Eddie O'Sullivan, lived in Kensal Road with six sisters, and they always used to go back to Ireland. We went back to Ireland maybe once or twice a year. We would go back at Christmas and maybe one week in the summer.

I went on a Country Holidays Fund holiday when I was at St Andrew's. They sent me down to Exeter for two weeks to stay with a family. It was really brilliant because children didn't get holidays then. The money wasn't around. We all went to Paddington station and we all got in the same train. There were loads of us from all over the borough. When we arrived, someone would say, 'I'll have him,' or 'I'll take those two,' so I ended up with this nice family who had two little boys, one was my age, one was a bit younger. I stayed there for two weeks and it was fantastic. They took us to the seaside and the dad took us to football at St James' Park. That was my first ever football match and I think I was about 10. I only went once. I think you got it only the year before you left primary school. I think you had to pay something really small like two and six.

✑ Bob Crawley:

I never went on holiday with my parents or other family members. I don't even recall having day trips to the seaside. My escape to more exciting experiences and travel was through the Scouts, the 66th Kensington troop based at the top end of Kensal Road towards Ladbroke Grove. We had an old hut with a small parcel of land as the Scout HQ and I spent some weekends camping there and occasionally going to Gilwell Park, a major scouting HQ and campsite in Epping Forest.

The Scouts took me abroad for the first time to Sweden for three weeks by train all the way. Twenty of us went over. It was £30 but my mum and dad couldn't afford it, so I worked in the shoe shop under Hazlewood Tower to earn the money to go. We went by ferry from Dover to Calais and then by train to Hamburg. We stayed in a hostel overnight in Hamburg and then continued our journey to Sweden. It was a huge adventure. Most of us had never been out of Britain before. I couldn't even afford to buy a rucksack, so I bought an old kit bag, which cost me ten and six. Everyone else had rucksacks and I was carrying this big white kit bag on my shoulder. I was also carrying an axe. We all had knives on our waists, going across Europe armed to the teeth.

We went to stay with a Swedish family in a farmhouse for a night for dinner. The bloke drove us there driving like a maniac down dirt tracks. They gave us big slices of Ryvita-type bread, almost forcing it down our throats when we were looking for a bit of Hovis. We set up camp and entertained Swedish Scouts, honing our outdoor skills like fire lighting, building shelters, tying knots and orienteering. We all took turns cooking over the camp fire. I got pulled over by the police in the middle of nowhere for walking across the road in the wrong place when there wasn't a car in sight. Every day though, the police would come to the campsite to make sure we were OK. It was in 1967, the year Sweden changed over from driving on the left to driving on the right. As we went round, we could see all the new signs covered up ready for the changeover day. One day everyone drove on the left and the next day they had to come out their houses and drive on the right.

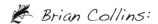 *Brian Collins:*

Two times when I was a little boy, we went to Ireland on a family visit for a week. Once, I went with my older brother, so it was just the two of us. We were dropped off at Paddington station and managed to get to Rosslare in Ireland, where we were picked up by our relations. Those trips were very few and far between.

At St Francis' Junior School, they took us on a bus to the seaside once a year and no one played truant that day. They would take us to Littlehampton and for some boys that would be their only trip to the seaside all year. It was a real treat for us. After my uncle and aunt moved to Maidenhead, my parents would ask them if they could put me up for a few days sometimes so they would take me to Paddington station as maybe a 10-year-old and put me on a train to Maidenhead. My Uncle Michael would be waiting at the other end. They had a house with a garden. I thought this was like heaven, a lovely little town by the river where I would play with my cousins. It was lovely down there for a few days.

There was the opportunity to go camping in St Mary's Bay in Kent in the summer with the youth club, where they owned property. They had a couple of acres down there. There were designated weeks and so there was a family week when parents and their young children had a particular week in July or August, but the highlight for us was the youth club week when we could go down there and create merry hell. It was right on the beach, so we could swim and go socialising. We would get up to all sorts, go a bit crazy and do the sort of things that W10 boys do but it was lovely for us because our families couldn't afford a holiday, so that would be one week a year when we could go to the seaside. There was a local working men's club, which we would fill every night, so we brought a lot of business down there.

eleven

Headline News

 *Frank Hale:*

My dad was too old to go in the forces in the war so he was called up to the fire service on the barges on the Thames. My two brothers were too young to go in the forces, so my eldest brother used to help out the air-raid wardens. We all had gas masks and kids had masks with a tongue on it so the mask looked like Mickey Mouse. We had an air-raid shelter in our back garden, or sometimes we used to go to Notting Hill Gate underground station to shelter. When I was about 3, Convent Gardens at the back of us was bombed. We were under the table in our house because there was an air raid on and there was a terrific bang and all the windows shattered in our house. After another raid, there was a sweet shop in Portobello Road got bombed and we were picking up all the melted chocolate. We used to collect shrapnel. You could exchange that for American comics like *Superman*. Swapping was a big thing. The war didn't seem real, more like a game. It was exciting and I couldn't wait to go out in the morning and see what I could forage for. We didn't have any sense of danger. One day we thought we were helping to demolish the bombed houses and a whole wall came down and just missed us.

There was a woman up Westbourne Park Road who used to repair clothes or cut down and alter clothes. One day, my mum measured me up and went up there and gave her a pair of my older brother's trousers to cut down. The woman said to come back next week. When we went back, the street had all been bombed and the woman had been killed. I looked up to my mum and said, 'Does that mean we've lost our sixpence?' I was only 5 or 6. Never mind about that poor woman, I was more worried about the sixpence.

We used to watch the airplanes fighting over the Scrubs and there used to be quite a few come down. We would climb all over them and get inside if we could until they shooed us off. The bombing got so bad, my grandad wrote to Mrs Stone in Letchmore Heath, where he lodged when he was younger, and asked her if I could stay there. The lady that my mum worked for had a big American Buick and she picked me up and drove me all the way from our house to Mrs Stone's with my mum and dad. All of a sudden, they went and I'm left on my own with this woman. She had a lodger, a strange woman wearing a big leather glove sliding down the stairs on her bum. I was bloody terrified. Mrs Stone was a hard woman with a wart on her chin. Her husband died when she was young and she was hardened. She

Party in Rillington Place to celebrate VJ Day, Victory over Japan, marking the end of the Second World War, August 1945. The infamous Christie murders in Rillington Place overshadow the fact that the street was a close-knit community like most streets in North Kensington. The street no longer exists as the road layout was changed following redevelopment in the 1970s.

wasn't used to kids and she was strict. She gave me a bath and whacked me with a wet towel when I cried.

I only knew Notting Hill before and suddenly I was in this little two-bedroomed cottage in a beautiful village next to a farm. Mrs Stone took me up to the farm and introduced me and I helped out by doing jobs like herding the cows up to the field and collecting them. There were two prisoners of war at Warren's Farm and one of them taught me to drive a

Children, including Roger Rogowski (light-coloured shorts), in Edenham Street watch the hunt for the weapon that killed Kelso Cochrane, May 1959. Kelso Cochrane was stabbed about 100 yards from this spot on the corner of Golborne Road and Southam Street. Hazlewood Crescent, now completely redeveloped, is in the background while Trellick Tower occupies the site of Edenham Street.

horse and cart. I went to the village school but I was like an alien to them. I was the only Londoner and no one would talk to me for a long time. When we broke up for the summer holidays, I would go out on my own and walk for miles over the fields. I got to learn about nature. There was a lovely little village pond and Mrs Stone had this enormous Victoria plum tree with the most gorgeous plums ever. Mrs Stone had a couple of cats and whenever they had kittens, she would put them in a sack, tie the sack up and put them in the water butt. I saw her do it one day so I took them out but she clumped me round the ear and put them back.

My mum and dad stayed in London and visited after two months and come down on the bus. It took half a day to get there changing buses, then you had to walk 2 miles across a field to get to the village. When I came back home for a week, I brought back a suitcase full of conkers and swapped them with my friends because they were hard to come by. We used to try to collect them from Hyde Park but the police would stop us and send us back because we were ragamuffins. I finally came home for good and spent the rest of the war in Notting Hill. I was watching the doodlebugs come over one sunny day. It must have been August towards the end of the war. One came over, a noisy bloody thing flying not very high with an orange flame coming out the back. It came over Convent Gardens and stopped and we started running in all directions. It came down at an angle and fell in Blenheim Crescent, or over that way, with an almighty bang.

I nearly drowned in Convent Gardens when I was about 8. There was a large concrete water tank so water was available for the fire service. It was 12 metres by 6 and 2 metres deep, with barbed wire round the top to stop kids falling in. I climbed up to get our football, slipped on the sloping sides and went under. I managed to grab hold of the barbed wire and Mrs Sayers pulled me out.

I remember the VE Day party when everyone came out to celebrate and everyone was very jolly. They set out tables and chairs in Westbourne Park Road and closed the road off for the day, and there was all food on the table. Just after coronation, I was waiting for the Queen to drive past at the bus stop at the bottom of Westbourne Park Road. There was a parade of cars come down the road and her car stopped just outside the bus stop, literally only about 5 foot away, and she smiled at me.

☾ Jane Traies:

The local Conservative Party headquarters was in Ladbroke Grove. It had a shop front. Our Auntie Joy was leafleting for them in the 1950 election year. We were to go inside to collect the leaflets one night and somehow in the general scrum we all came out and my little cousin, who was 18 months old, was shut inside, so someone had to find a phone to call someone to open up again.

Our granny wanted to see the King when he died but she worked a flanker because she got her very old and infirm auntie up from the country and she wrote to the palace to say, 'I want to see the King but my auntie can't stand all that time,' so they replied and she got to the front of the queue. There was a huge street party in St Lawrence Terrace in 1953 for the coronation. All the girls had red, white and blue ribbons in their hair and we all sat at long tables all the way down St Lawrence Terrace. I remember I wanted to go to the loo, so a lady took me into her house into the bathroom where I saw something I'd never seen before. It was a real sponge. We were taken out to sit on the pavement to see the Queen drive by. She visited all parts of London in a big black car. We were taken as a primary school class to stand by the side of the road. We were terribly excited. We were taught to make our own Union Jacks on a stick to wave when the Queen went by. We stood on the pavement deciding what to say or what to shout out but she went by and if you blinked you missed it and she was gone.

We weren't brought up with any politics. Our parents were shopkeepers who thought Winston Churchill had done a good job so they voted Conservative. The first time I heard one of my school friends slagging off Winston Churchill I was shocked. It was like saying something about God. Nobody told us who Mosley was or what was going on.

☾ Margaret Burdsey (née Traies):

I used to go up to St Lawrence Terrace and play two balls against the wall in the evening with my friends and my mum would sometimes say, 'You're not going out tonight because there's a Mosley meeting.' I don't remember the politics behind it but we were frightened of the black people. In 1959, I was 10. We didn't have black children at school then because they were almost all working men in the area. A lot of the riots went on largely round All Saints but there was that one occasion when there was a riot and it spilled out along Ladbroke Grove.

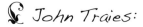 John Traies:

The race riots were a big thing. After our dad divided our bedroom in Chesterton Road, a bottle was thrown through our bedroom window and our mum took us into their bedroom at the back. There was one particularly bad night. The shop window was smashed as well. There was 'Mosley' written in big white letters on the side of Wornington Road School for a long time. I didn't know what it was so I asked my mum and she said, 'It's just some silly man.'

When Winston Churchill died in 1965, our Uncle Billy went to pay homage to 'the great man', in his words. He liked a drink, Billy, and he went with his mate Ronnie Price and they got in the queue, which went right over Westminster Bridge and was miles long. They spent about six hours in the queue and he had to go to the loo so he went but then he had to join the back of the queue again, so he was there all day.

Maureen Rafferty (née Coker):

When we had the coronation party in 1953, Beryl Woodgate was the queen. She lived at No. 15. Bobby Rudge lived at No. 5 and he was the king and I was behind holding the crown, which my dad made where he worked at St Charles' Hospital. The crown was all made out of plaster of Paris. My dad collected the money for the party and organised games, and we got given a pen with a crown on as a present. Golborne Gardens had their own street party.

Gwen Nelson (née Martin):

King George VI died in February 1952, not long before we moved to Golborne Road. There was public mourning as he had been a popular monarch, especially as a result of his visits with the Queen Mother to the worst bombed parts of London during the war. Men had black patches sewn onto their coat sleeves and women wore a jet brooch if they had one. After the funeral, there was the coronation of the new monarch. The coronation was to take place on 2 June 1953 and a neighbourhood committee was formed to organise events to mark the occasion. Although the war ended in 1945, sugar, butter, cheese and cooking fats were still rationed. To mark the coronation, the government allowed everyone an extra pound of sugar, 4oz of margarine and derationed eggs. Bakers were allowed extra fat. Street parties were held throughout Britain. Ours was in Golborne Gardens between the Prince Arthur and the bomb site. Trestle tables and wooden benches were borrowed from local churches and halls. Red, white and blue bunting was hung from windows and everyone was issued with an official invitation to the party. I think the party was on the weekend before the coronation.

Everyone dressed in their Sunday best, Boys in grey serge suits with knee-length shorts, shoes well-polished and hair slicked down with Brylcreem. Girls wore party frocks adorned with red, white and blue ribbons if they had them, or dressed up like a queen in one of their mums' old nighties and a paper crown. It was a warm day. A local brass band churned out patriotic music, 'Hearts of Oak', 'Rule Britannia', 'Land of Hope and Glory'. We had never seen tables piled so high with food, although it was mostly white bread sandwiches with a Spam or Heinz Sandwich Spread filling. There were also trifles and jellies and a multi-tiered cake with tricolour icing. To drink, there were huge pitchers of cordial. The adults fortified themselves with beer or shandy from the Arthur, or cups of tea.

Each child was given a coronation mug or cup and saucer and there was a clown to entertain us. The reason I feel our party was earlier than the coronation is because, on the day, we went to my father's cousins who lived in Shirland Road to watch the event on their television. We were all dressed in our best. Dad was in his Harris tweed suit, complete with waistcoat and Mum wore a floral summer dress, fur stole and feather fascinator. I was dressed in party clothes and patent leather shoes with silver buckles, given strict instructions to sit still and not do anything for fear of getting dirty. Few people had television in 1953 and this was my first experience of one. It was a large wooden cabinet with a grey glass window about 9 inches across and 6 inches high. It took several minutes after being switched on to warm up and a black and white screen appear. Dining chairs were arranged in front of the box as if in a cinema and, when a programme came on, it was given your full attention. We stood for the National Anthem, then perched attentively. From the moment we first heard Richard Dimbleby's tones, we were mesmerised. After it finished, tea and sandwiches and Victoria sponge were served, then it was time to go home. As it was a mild evening and we'd been sitting for several hours, my parents decided to walk down Elgin Avenue to Harrow Road, where we turned onto Great Western Road and then onto Kensal Road. As we crossed over to go down Kensal Road, Dad stopped. 'What's that in the gutter?' He bent to pick it up. It was a man's Wittnauer watch with a gold strap. Dad took it to Harrow Road police station but it was never claimed and returned to him. He always wore it and even today, years later, it's still going.

Jeannie Rowe (née Searson):

The year 1953 was very significant. In June, the queen was crowned. We didn't have a television or access to one. On the actual day, we were travelling by coach from Scotland to London. I think we must have got all our information from the newspapers. At school we were each given a souvenir. My sister got a coronation mug and a teaspoon with a crown on the top. I got a purple tin, which had a bar of chocolate in. The colour of the tin was Cadbury's purple, so maybe they sponsored them. There was a royal decoration on the tin. A few days before, the conquest of Everest took place. This was also much publicised and we were taken as a school to watch a film about it at the local cinema.

Charlie Phillips:

The community was stronger then, because people looked out for each other, black and white, but outsiders would come in to try to disrupt it. It got so bad they used to accuse us that we had twenty people living in a house but we never had nowhere to go. Oswald Mosley used to keep his meetings right outside that house in Blenheim Crescent. It was firebombed when it was attacked by teddy boys. There was a few black families living in All Saints Road and one of them opened a little cafeteria and Mosley would be outside having meetings. St Michael's was the church the Kelso Cochrane funeral took place but I wasn't allowed to go that afternoon but I watched it from the street. It was one of the biggest funerals I've seen.

The start of the carnival is very debatable but I was there to see the first one on the street. It wasn't called carnival then. I was in Portobello Road and I heard this commotion and I came out and photographed it. It was a group of people who marched round the streets. It was organised by Rhaune Laslett, who used to live in Tavistock Road. There was a steel band playing. Mrs Laslett rented a lorry and they had kids on the lorry, and they just drove round the block, Tavistock Road, Portobello Road, Lancaster Road, All Saints Road, and that was it. There's another side of it where Claudia Jones started it in Kings Cross.

 *Vee Davis:*

The teddy boy riot. That was '58. It had that thing they call the smog so the place is dark, you are dark, and you're wondering who is behind you because you don't know, you can't see faces, because no matter how white you are, you can't see the faces and sometimes you bump into people and say sorry.

I was at Osram at the time, leaving Osram's, getting off at Ladbroke Grove station and I remember this gang of blackers, because I never see so many blacks in this area, but it was a gang of blackers and I think they were all from Brixton. I didn't know the place called Brixton and I remember, as I came out of the station, they were there and just shouting, 'Go home and pray for your brothers. Just go home and lock up. Don't come out,' you know, for they had come up to fight the teddy boys, because around this area we didn't have so much blacks to fight them. I was living in Colville Terrace there, in Rachman house. I remember coming out from the station and walking fast to get into the house. Well, you don't know, you're scared, like you don't want nothing to come behind you or too close on you, and you just keep your eyes straight, you don't looking at nobody and you're trying to get in as fast as possible.

And then once we in, I remember this same friend, who had just arrived in this country, she was so scared. We had a big old Rachman wardrobe, we used to be pushing it every night against the door. During the day you'd hear them pass and say things like, 'That's a nigger lover house.' It had a blonde chick who used to live down there, Reenie, and she really liked the black men. I guess they used to watch and see, so they used to call it a nigger lover house. 'We're coming to get that tonight' and stuff like that, whether they come or not, they say it and it make you scared. I think when they finish with us down here, the fascists started in East London, remember they used to beat up the Pakis and the Jews in East London.

Pearl Prescod had a march from Ladbroke Grove station to the American Embassy. I'd just had my little boy, I think he was a few months old, so I would still be breastfeeding him, but I went in and I said to my husband there's a march going on there, I won't be long, I just want to go and see. So he said OK but I ended up in the American Embassy. This was a peace march, like 'We shall overcome', in '63. They were having problems in America with the same black and white thing, 'You black you stay at the back' and stuff like that. It was for this black awareness stuff, everybody who believed it wasn't fair, whether they're black or white or whatever, who thought the whole system was corrupted with this. The colour of your skin mattered so much, so everybody was marching, black and white. It was happening in America and they brought it over here. We're all going through the same thing, we're all getting the same problem, so they marched. I don't want to be African, leave religion out, I'm just me.

❧ *Margaret Stedman (née Riddick):*

We were in Lancaster Road when the Notting Hill riots happened. I was walking to Kensal Road and the police said, 'You've got to be off the street at nine o'clock.' There was trouble on the corner of Southam Street and Golborne Road, and two policemen went into the phone box by the bridge. They came out later and said they were making a phone call but we reckon they were hiding.

❀ *Ray Matthews:*

I clearly remember the riots and the awful scary time as kid. I didn't understand it all and to me then black people were to be avoided and it was OK to abuse them. My dad never went out at night during that time without carrying a carving knife to protect himself.

Alan Peverall:

I can't remember the Notting Hill riots but I remember the film crews in Southam Street and by the police box next to the iron bridge. That was for the murder of Kelso Cochrane that followed the riots.

Reg Thackeray:

My dad told me Holm's used have a sign saying 'German bread' in the window and it was broken during the war. I remember when the West Indians started coming in. The first one I ever saw I said to my mum, 'Look there's a golliwog,' because I'd never seen one before. She was embarrassed. I remember the signs in windows saying 'No blacks, no Irish and no dogs'. I remember the riots. Fighting started down Latimer Road way and, down Portobello, a lot of the shop windows were all smashed in, including Wolfy Marks' wallpaper shop, Shepherd's the funeral director and Tommy Little's sweet shop.

Roger Rogowski:

I remember hearing on the grapevine about the race riots of 1958 as a 5-year-old but I'd completely forgotten about the murder of Kelso Cochrane, which happened the following year, so I was amazed to see a photo of myself on the cover of Mark Olden's book and in a report in the *Daily Mirror* from that time, so I was out on the street as a 6-year-old watching the police hunting for the murder weapon. I remember asking my parents about some fight that I'd heard about and they explained it away as being a party and some people dancing in the street, so I'm sure the two were linked.

Also, in about the early 1960s, the exploits of Peter Rachman in Notting Hill were becoming widely known but my parents considered themselves lucky to have the gentlemanly Mr Sohacki for a landlord, who allowed my dad to chop up his old furniture and decorate our flat more or less as he pleased.

 *Brian Collins:*

I'm still saddened that I didn't see the Beatles being filmed in my street when they made that film, *A Hard Day's Night*, because we were only a short way away. Our school finished and we just left school in Blechynden Street and met some mates from another school outside who said they'd just seen the Beatles. They said they've been filming by St John's School in Clarendon Road. All of us boys, there must have been fifty of us, shot along the road under the railway bridge at Latimer Road station shrieking and shouting like crazy people. We got there as quickly as possible and, when we got to St John's School, you could see them clearing stuff away. We'd just missed them. It grieves me that Richard Lester cut the scene where the Beatles went in the Portland. You can see stills in books but I've never seen it in film. They also filmed *The Knack* in the Portland.

Susan Mcmahon:

My mum loved Paul McCartney. She saw them filming the Beatles by the burnt-out church in St Luke's Road, so she went outside to have a look but she was so long, she burnt my dad's dinner and he went mad.

twelve

All Change

∾ Frank Hales:

Eventually we did move out of Notting Hill when I was 15, in 1953. My dad put an advert in the paper. He was a painter and decorator and offered to do £300 worth of work in exchange for a house. Someone in Bromley answered. Their parents had died and left a beautiful house that was a bit derelict, so my dad did it up. It was in Bromley Common and the area was a little bit posh.

Ken Farrow:

I was working for Saxone shoes in Oxford Street in 1968. I took a sickie one day and went for a walk round London and found myself going past Australia House in the Strand and, just out of curiosity, I picked up some brochures about going to Australia. I was sitting in the kitchen that night looking at the brochures. My mum said if you even think about going to Australia, I'll never talk to you again so that was it. I was working in the Feathers in Dalgarno Way one day and one of the blokes there said, 'You don't have the guts to go to Australia,' so he bet me ten Weights I wouldn't go. I ended up in Australia and I still haven't got my cigarettes. When I came back to the UK for a visit he'd died, so he never paid up, the bugger. They told me at Australia House I would be welcome with open arms. By then, I had a degree in social work and I'd been working part-time in social work for nine years. They told me there was no need to apply for a job here, I'd pick one up when I get there. When I got there, they said you'll have to start training all over again. They wanted me to go back to school and take their equivalent to O-levels.

🐚 Margaret Burdsey (née Traies):

In 1975, our parents lost their lease on their shop in Ladbroke Grove. The landlord didn't renew the lease on their shop. They went to court to try and contest the decision, the fact that they'd had the lease for so long. The landlord wanted to develop that whole corner. They had no work. They were lucky they had a house in Angmering, otherwise they would have been homeless as well.

🌿 Pauline Clark (née Harding):

My brothers and sisters all started their married life in the top two rooms at 10 Bosworth Road, then they all moved away to Langley, Salisbury, Sunbury and Plumstead. I moved to Ashford at the age of 15.

Acklam Road looking east from Portobello Road just before the Westway was opened in July 1970. The houses to the left were later demolished following protests by residents.

New replacing old in Appleford Road looking towards Bosworth Road, 1969. All of the old buildings including St Andrew's School, to the left, and Davis' the cleaner's, indicated by the tall chimney, were demolished later, except the Earl Derby, which still stands having been converted into flats.

Jean Russell (née Hemming):

My partner came to my mum's house after I left him, kicking the door, so I moved to Brighton but he broke into my sister's house and found the address and came to Brighton. I finally went to the police after he beat me again. I was beaten and cut so badly I looked like a piece of liver. I kidnapped my sons from school and took them home to my mum. I went to the welfare and they gave me a place in Hackney. It was a place for the homeless, where they filmed *Cathy Come Home*. It was full of cockroaches. I had a room like a cell with iron beds. Because I and my boys looked nice, they only kept me in for a weekend and they put me in a halfway house. There was a supervisor. If you pay your rent and look after your children properly they give you a flat and I got a flat in Deptford. That was the end of my life in Ladbroke Grove.

Derek Ford:

We left Chesterton Road in June or July 1958 and moved to a brand new flat in Roehampton. We had a balcony so Dad started growing geraniums and we stayed there until 1973, then they moved further down the road to Barnes Common. When we moved to Roehampton, they couldn't find a school for me in Putney or Roehampton, so I travelled on the bus and train back to Isaac Newton in the first year. I was there for nearly a year before they found me a place at a local school.

Gwen Nelson (née Martin):

The 1960s were times of change in North Kensington. Hazlewood and Adair Towers were built and the other side of Golborne Road rebuilt as shops and a library. It was only a matter of time before the other side would be demolished and decisions made by my parents about what they wanted to do. They were reluctant to take up the council offer of a flat as it would have only been a two-bedroom one in a high-rise block and we'd been used to having all the rooms above Mum's shop, the basement and backyard.

Keith was back in Newcastle in August 1966 and I was awaiting the start of the academic year, having already given up my job, so I went up to spend time with him. He and another student were sharing a flat, so this was the first time I had actually been with him away from his overprotective mother. We decided we would become engaged with the thought of marrying once he'd completed his apprenticeship and I my course. I phoned home to let my parents know which train I was catching and that I had something to tell them. I arrived back in Golborne Road bubbling with excitement to tell Mum and Dad that Keith and I were going to get married but before I had a chance to say anything, Mum said, 'Your Dad and I have decided we are going to New Zealand. You can come with us. We'll pay your fare or we will leave enough money to support you for a year.' She also said that my Aunt Micky and her husband had also decided to go to New Zealand, where their youngest sister lived after having married a New Zealand soldier at the end of the war. They'd all managed to get tickets on the same ship, the *Orcades*. I was gobsmacked as there had never been any mention of emigrating before I went to stay with Keith. Still in shock, I went upstairs with my case, came down and, in panic, said I would go to New Zealand with them.

❧ Margaret Stedman (née Riddick):

The Notting Hill Trust bought the house that I lived in in Lancaster Road, and that's how I moved out to Camberley in the 1970s.

❀ Ray Matthews:

We had to move out in 1965 as the rooms we had were condemned as unfit and overcrowded, so we moved to Bermondsey. We had a brand new flat with a proper kitchen, a bathroom and hot water and, for the first time, we could have a fridge. My darling mum was so happy.

❦ Babs Coker:

We moved to Hounslow as they were knocking down all the houses in Acklam Road to make way for the motorway, which went right over our house. I still travelled from our new house in Hounslow to school because my dad still worked in W10, so he took me and then I met him from work and he brought me home.

❧ Alan Peverall:

I never left the area. I've seen so many changes and not all of them for the better. It's hard to imagine what it used to be like but I still think of growing up in Southam Street. I loved it.

❦ Marg Pithers:

My nan and grandad moved to Harlesden and we moved out to Streatham in 1968. By then, there was four children and my brother was 2 years old. None of our family are in the area now.

✒ Roger Rogowski:

Like a lot of parents in the area I suppose, mine wanted something better for themselves and their growing sons. Even before my brother was born, I recall my parents talking about emigrating to Australia as it was possible to go then on an assisted package for £10. My mum's uncle and aunt and their families had emigrated and settled in Melbourne after the war, and my dad had already effectively emigrated from Poland, so this was a realistic possibility. One day we went to Australia House in the Strand to get more information but, for whatever reason, they decided not to follow it up.

A lot of the streets on the west side of Golborne Road between the railway and the canal had been demolished and redeveloped by the mid-Sixties, and then it was our turn as everything on the opposite side of Golborne Road was going to be demolished to make way for Trellick Tower. Dad had the option to relocate from his office in Carnwath Road to a new one in central Croydon, so one day in early July 1966, between England's last group match in the World Cup and the quarter-final against Argentina, in a less dramatic move than emigrating to Australia, we moved to Croydon.

🐾 Mossy Condon:

We moved out of Hazlewood Tower to Holmfield House in 1969 and we stayed there until 1971, and then we moved to Kensal Green, and then I moved back again and bought the Derby in September 1993, and I had it until March 2010. My dad had died by then and I wish I'd been able to serve him a pint in there after he'd been refused service all those years ago. Now they've turned it into flats because the brewery sold the building. They wanted £2 million for it.

🦋 Barbara Reynolds (née Murray):

When people started moving away, I lost touch with a lot of them but always stayed friends with the Ingarfields. Some of them just went. There was no goodbyes or anything or it was just 'We're moving tomorrow'. I moved out the area in 1973 when I got married and I moved to Southfields.

✒ Bob Crawley:

We moved to Hazlewood Tower after the council said our flat in Bosworth House was too big once my sister married and left home, and then we moved to Trellick Tower, flat 18 on the third floor. A big drawback for the area was that, as the rebuilding in the area grew larger, our friends and extended family members moved further away, mainly out to West London, and contact became less and less. Many of us had to move much further out when we wanted to set up home as it was expensive to buy locally and getting a council place was out of the question unless you had sufficient points for the council housing list, and priority was given to people with kids or those who could play the system by such ploys as getting pregnant or pretending that you were being evicted by your parents. When I got married, I moved to Royal Oak and then to Irchester in Northamptonshire.

✒ Brian Collins:

In the mid-Sixties, my uncle and aunt had the opportunity to move out to Maidenhead when the slum clearance was going on and people were being rehoused, but my dad was very resistant to moving out. There were six of us by then and we'd taken over the house. We had a lodger on the top floor who worked on the railways because we couldn't afford the rent for all of it, so we never had the house in its entirety but my dad still wouldn't move out. Whenever we visited our relations in Stepney and Bow, when it was time to go, my dad's parting comment was, 'It's time to go back to the Royal Borough.' He loved it where we lived. He loved the buzz of the area and the markets.

✒ Susan Mcmahon:

We moved out in 1968 when they started knocking it all down. We moved to the Avenues in Paddington.

Landmarks and Language Glossary

Not all of the landmarks listed were or are in Notting Hill or North Kensington but they were well-known to people who lived there.

area – sometimes shortened to 'airy', the small courtyard below street level in front of the basement of a terraced house. Basement flats could be damp and prone to flooding but they usually had the small benefit of at least having a private front door, where the flats above would have a shared front door, staircase and passageways. Basement flats usually had sole access to the coal cellar, if there was one, and the backyard.

Amberley Road School – opened in 1881, it became Amberley Primary and Kemble Secondary School in 1951 before becoming North Paddington Secondary Modern Upper School for boys and girls with the Lower School in Harrow Road. The site is now occupied by flats with ARK Atwood Primary Academy on the ground floor.

Arthur – the Prince Arthur, a pub on the corner of Golborne Road and Golborne Gardens, which is now a restaurant.

Avenues, The – local name for the Queen's Park estate in Paddington, so named after the succession of roads running north off Harrow Road, First to Sixth Avenues.

bagwash – a forerunner of fully automated launderettes, clothes were taken to the bagwash in a large canvas or cotton bag to be washed by staff for collection later, when the wet washing would be taken home to be dried and ironed. Clothes were almost always washed in the bag but they were sometimes taken out of the bag. Washing could also be returned dry but many saved the additional cost and dried their clothes at home.

Barlby Road Primary School – the original building was on the site occupied by the current school building.

BDH – British Drug Houses, which occupied 222 Kensal Road, one of the rare original buildings that still exist in Kensal Road.

Beehive – a pub at the junction of Walmer Road and Talbot Grove demolished in the 1960s and now the site of the Kensington Sports Centre.

Blenheim Crescent (No. 9) – the ground floor was occupied by Totobags Café, which was the scene of serious violence in August 1958 during the Notting Hill riots.

bomb site – also referred to as 'debris', the sites may or may not have been fenced off but it made little difference to determined children. There were plenty of them in post-war London and they were unofficial, if sometimes dangerous, playgrounds.

Brit – the Britannia, a pub that stood on the corner of Kensal Road and Golborne Road before being demolished to make way for Trellick Tower. There were two other pubs in the area called the Britannia, respectively at 217 Latimer Road, which was demolished to make way for the Westway, and at 125 Clarendon Road, which is now a restaurant. There is a fourth Britannia at 1 Allen Street in nearby W8, which still exists. None of the stories in this book relate to these three pubs.

bug'ole, bughole, bug house – sometimes also known as the fleapit, this cinema was officially called the Imperial. Located in Portobello Road, it later became the Electric.

Cardinal Manning School – Cardinal Manning Boys' School was opened in 1955 and Cardinal Manning Girl's School in 1958. The girls' school merged with the Sisters of Sion School in Bayswater to form the present-day Sion-Manning School and the boys' school became St Charles Catholic Sixth Form College.

Carnarvon – The Carnarvon Castle, a pub on the corner of Portobello Road and Golborne Road, which is now a restaurant.

Carlton Bridge Tavern – a pub by Carlton Bridge on Great Western Road, which later became the Union Tavern.

Children's Country Holidays Fund – established in 1884 by Reverend Samuel Barnett and his wife Henrietta and originally called The Children's Fresh Air Mission, the charity's aim was to take children from London's slums away for holidays in the fresh air and country surroundings. In 1886 the name changed to The Children's Country Holidays Fund.

clippie – bus conductress.

Cobden Club – a members' club at 170-172 Kensal Road, now a private house. The Cobden Club and Working Men's Institute was opened in 1880 and named after Richard Cobden, a prominent reformer.

Coliseum – a cinema that stood at 324 Harrow Road before being demolished to make way for housing. Sometimes referred to as The Coli.

Cut, The – the Grand Union Canal.

Derby – The Earl Derby, a pub on the corner of Southern Row and Bosworth Road, later converted into flats.

Essoldo – a cinema that stood at 22 Great Western Road and later became the Zig Zag Club before being demolished to make way for housing.

Feathers – the Seven Feathers was a community centre in Edenham Street comprising a day nursery, youth club and pensioners' club. It was one of a number of clubs run by The Feathers Clubs Association, which was founded in 1934 by Mrs Freda Dudley Ward, a friend of the Prince of Wales, who became King Edward VIII. The Prince of Wales allowed his crest of three feathers to be used as the insignia of the association. Initially formed to aid those suffering in the Depression of the 1930s, the Feathers Association moved into youth and community work after the Second World War.

Florence Gladstone School – see Wornington Road School.

Foresters – the Foresters Arms stood on the corner of West Row and Southern Row before being demolished to make way for housing.

Frenchies – shortened version of the old colloquial name for condoms, French letters.

gab – sometimes called the gift of the gab, the ability to talk confidently and persuasively.

gaff – a house or home.

Golborne Road chapel – at 92 Golborne Road, converted into offices in 2003, this former chapel also operated as a sanctuary for ex-prisoners from Wormwood Scrubs prison in the post-war period.

Hamperl's – a popular butcher's shop that occupied No. 80 Golborne Road.

Ha'penny steps – the footbridge linking Kensal Road via Wedlake Street and Harrow Road, originally opened as a toll bridge in the 1880s, replaced in 1905 and later replaced with a pram- and bike-friendly bridge.

Hazlewood Tower – was completed in 1962 at the same time as Adair Tower. The site on which the tower now stands was a popular bombsite for children after the war, when it was cleared following the demolition of St Andrew's and St Philip's Church, which originally stood on the site.

Holm's – a baker's shop that stood on the corner of Golborne Road and Wornington Road. Bread was baked on the premises. The Holm family owned a second property on the corner of Golborne Road and Swinbrook Road, where cakes were baked and decorated.

jerker – a plank swing, which was a standard piece of playground equipment. The plank could accommodate several children seated with bolder children standing on the plank at either end hanging on to the supporting arms.

jumping jacks – a small firework with a series of small charges of gunpowder packed into a multiple 's' configuration. When lit, they produced a series of loud bangs while being propelled in random directions along the ground. Not surprisingly, they were later banned on safety grounds but there were great fun at the time.

Kenilworth – the Kenilworth Castle stood at 104 St Anne's Road and was converted into a supermarket.

King's Troop – there are a few references to the mass of horse-drawn gun carriages that used to travel through North Kensington on a regular basis between their barracks in St John's Wood and Wormwood Scrubs.

Knitmaster – manufacturer of knitting machines that occupied a big red brick building at 96–100 Kensal Road, which stood where Meanwhile Gardens is located, between Trellick Tower and the canal.

Lads of the Village – a pub on the corner of Kensal Road and Middle Row, which later became Frames. Sometimes referred to as 'the Lads'.

Lancaster Road Baths – comprised a swimming pool, baths with hot and cold running water in cubicles, and facilities for washing clothes, the baths stood in Silchester Road on the site now occupied by Kensington Aldridge Academy. The Baths were very popular for people with no bathrooms at home who otherwise only had access to a portable tin bath, which was filled with hot and cold water from several pans or buckets and likewise emptied at the end.

(The) lane – Portobello Road, from when the road was known as Portobello Lane in the days when it ran from Notting Hill Gate to Portobello Farm, which stood about 300 yards north of the railway bridge.

Latimer Road mission – officially the Latymer Mission, which stood in Blechyden Street just off Latimer Road before being demolished and replaced by the Latymer Christian Centre in Bramley Road.

Little House – the Clayton Arms, which stood at 9 West Row before being demolished to make way for housing.

little rec – the Emslie Horniman Pleasance in East Row.

(I Was) Lord Kitchener's Valet – one of the early Sixties' boutiques, which occupied 293 Portobello Road.

Metropolitan Theatre – stood at 267 Edgware Road on a site now occupied by Paddington police station.

Mitre – there were two pubs called the Mitre in the area. One stood on the corner of Golborne Road and Wornington Road, which was demolished after a fire. The other one, on the corner of Holland Park Avenue and Ladbroke Grove, still exists.

navvies – short for navigational engineer, originally manual labourers working on major civil engineering projects and later, almost any manual labourer.

Newsreel – officially called the World's News Theatre and renamed the Classic in 1957, which stood at 5 Praed Street before being demolished to make way for offices.

North Paddington School – Mixed secondary modern school with its Upper school in Amberley Road and Lower School in Harrow Road. The Harrow Road site is now occupied by flats.

Odeon, Westbourne Grove – a smart post-war cinema that stood on the corner of Westbourne Grove and Chepstow Road before being demolished to make way for housing.

old money – this was the period before decimalisation when there were twelve pennies to a shilling and twenty shillings to a pound. There was a language of its own attached to old money. A sixpenny piece was a tanner, a shilling was a bob and two shillings and sixpence was half a crown. Two pence was always shortened to 'tuppence' and three pence was shortened to 'thrupence' or 'threpence', where the 'e' was pronounced as in 'end', and all other amounts of pennies were pronounced as one word not two distinct words as now. As now, amounts of money were shortened in speech to, for example, one pound ten, meaning one pound and ten shillings (£1 10s), while amounts of shillings and pence were shortened to, for example, seven and six, meaning seven shillings and sixpence (7s 6d).

Pelican – a pub on the corner of All Saints Road and Tavistock Road, now a bar.

penny drink – fizzy drinks were almost always sold in large bottles and, anyway, many children couldn't afford to buy a small bottle or can of drink even when they were available, so many shopkeepers would open a large bottle and sell it by the glass for a penny.

Percy – the Earl Percy stood on the corner of Ladbroke Grove and Chesterton Road and is now a boutique hotel.

pinny – short for pinafore, a type of full-length sleeveless and collarless dress worn over clothes to keep them clean.

Pisshouse – local name for the Colville, which stood on the corner of Portobello Road and Talbot Road, now a bar.

Portland – the Portland Arms stood at 119 Portland Road, now a beauty spa.

Portobello Road School – Built in 1876 and now Chepstow House School, behind the buildings in Lancaster Road and Portobello Road. In 1958, the building was occupied by Isaac Newton Boys' Lower School with the Upper School in Wornington Road. A former entrance to the school in Portobello Road is now a shopping arcade.

Prince – the Prince of Wales stood at 48 Southern Row at the junction with Middle Row, now a bar/restaurant.

rag fair – a weekly Sunday market for second-hand goods that ran until before the Second World War in Bangor Street. The market was closed by the local council refusing to grant licences to the traders and the market moved to Portobello Road to become the second-hand goods section of that market. The street was demolished in the 1950s to make way for Henry Dickens Court.

Robin Hood and Little John – a pub that stood on the corner of Kensal Road and Southam Street before being demolished to make way for Trellick Tower. Sometimes referred to as 'the Robin Hood'.

Roman Catholic Church – there are some references to the church on the corner of Bosworth Road and Hazlewood Crescent, which is the Church of Our Lady of the Holy Souls, which still stands today.

Rugby Club – a youth club in Walmer Road. Founded by Arthur Walrond in 1884, it received the support of Rugby School in 1889 when the Headmaster, Dr Percival, decided that the school should undertake some social work in a major city. The club still operates as the Rugby Portobello Trust in Walmer Road.

Prince of Wales – a cinema that stood at 331 Harrow Road and hosted the ABC Minors, a weekly film programme for children, before being demolished to make way for housing.

Saga Records – a record manufacturer that occupied what is now Saga House at 326 Kensal Road and also occupied a smaller unit in a row of buildings where Holmfield House now stands in Kensal Road.

St Andrew's Primary School – built in 1874, a primary school, which stood on the railway side of the junction of Southam Street and Bosworth Road when the two streets used to meet. The school was known locally as the Doll's House because of its small size. The footprint of the old school and playground is now in St Thomas' School playground.

St Charles' Primary School – the original late nineteenth-century building was badly damaged by bombing in the war and was demolished and replaced by a new building in 1954.

St Francis' Primary School – the original building was replaced by a new school of the same name, St Francis of Assisi Primary School in Treadgold Street

St Helen's Church – the original nineteenth-century Anglican church was destroyed in the Second World War and rebuilt in the 1950s.

St Mark's Park – the park in St Mark's Road now known as Kensington Memorial Park.

St Mary's Catholic Primary School – this school is still thriving in its original nineteenth-century building in East Row.

St Michael's Church – St Michael and All Angels, which still stands on the corner of Ladbroke Grove and St Michael's Gardens.

(The) Scrubs – Wormwood Scrubs. Little Wormwood Scrubs on the east side of Scrubs Lane was always 'the little Scrubs'.

Shanty Town – the Shanty Town adventure playground was created by Rhaune Laslett's Notting Hill Neighbourhood Service around 1966 in the back gardens of the derelict houses awaiting demolition between Tavistock Crescent and Tavistock Road. A number of adventure playgrounds were created in the area from the 1950s onward to provide rare off-road spaces for children to play.

specky fruit – fruit that was over-ripe to the point of being bruised, often left behind by market stallholders as unsold and adopted as missiles by children.

synagogue – the Notting Hill Synagogue at 206–208 Kensington Park Road. The building is now occupied by a private members' gym.

Tavistock – the Tavistock Arms stood at 41 Tavistock Crescent on the corner of the alley leading to the footbridge over the railway before being demolished to make way for housing. Sometimes referred to as the Tavi.

tom – a prostitute.

totter – also known as rag and bone men or scrap men, they toured the streets, usually on a horse and cart, collecting unwanted household items to be sold on to scrap metal merchants and other dealers. Second-hand clothes were often sold at the northern end of Portobello market and in Golborne Road, and some families might even buy goods directly from the totter's cart. The characters in *Steptoe and Son* were based on totters in North Kensington.

(The) Town – Kensal Town, the area between the Grand Union Canal, the railway, Ladbroke Grove and Great Western Road. There was a historical, sometimes violent, rivalry between people from the Town, known as 'townies', and people from north of the canal.

tuppenny loose – inflation meant that the value could change but this meant a loose quantity of cigarettes from a packet split by the shopkeeper for people who couldn't afford a full packet of cigarettes at any one time. See 'old money'.

Warwick – the Earl of Warwick, a pub on the corner of Golborne Road and Southam Street, which is now a restaurant.

Wedlake – Wedlake Baths on the corner of Kensal Road and Wedlake Street comprised a swimming pool, baths with hot and cold running water in cubicles, and facilities for washing clothes, similar to Lancaster Road Baths.

Weston's Cider House – stood at 339 Harrow Road on the corner of Woodfield Place, before being demolished in 1970.

Whisky-A-Go-Go – a former night club based in Wardour Street in Soho, which opened in the early 1960s.

witch's hat – a conical metal frame balanced on a central pole, which was a standard piece of playground equipment before being banned. Children would hang on to the frame, causing it to swing around the central pole.

Wornington Road School – the building, erected in 1936 to replace the original school building from 1874, still exists as Kensington and Chelsea College. Wornington Road Infants' School occupied the site post-war and Florence Gladstone School for girls between the ages of 11 and 15, used also occupied the site from 1951. From 1958, the building was occupied by Isaac Newton Boys' Upper School, with the Lower School in Portobello Road.

Zetland – the Earl of Zetland stood at 116 Princedale Road, now offices.

Index

Picture entry signified by use of italics

List of Subscribers

Hannah Anderson
Linda Jane Atley

Annie Barazetti
Kathy Barazetti
Nathalie Ann Barazetti-Harris
The Bedwell family
John Bell
Thomas Bennett
Elaine Owen Blackall
Ian Blackman
Martin Botwright
Ted Burton
The Byrne family

Jane Carter
Yiannoula Christou
Sidney Albert Clifford
Babs Coker
Mossy Condon
Lady-Sarah Conlon
Mandy Coot
Audrey Counsell
Frederick and Jose Crawley

Carol and Thomas Dalton
Rehaanue (Rennie) Davis
Jim Dobrowski

Dave Eades
The Evans family
Dave and Joan Fisher
The Ford family

Eileen Galligan
Florence Goldsby
Joe Green

Jackie Hanson
Bill and Connie Harvey
The Harwood family
Michael Hollamby
Elaine Spencer Hopkins
Dave Hucker

Thomas Ireland

Steven Jeffery

Mick Kasmir
John and Betty Kenna

Albert Lapere
Vic and Gerry Martin
Rachel McCarthy
James McClenning
The McDermott family
Cornelius and Afreay Moroney
Barbara Murray

Bill Newman
Ann Norton

Pat Orridge

John William Pegg
The Pendry family
Agnes Ellen Powell

Samantha Reynolds
Rebecca Richardson
Frank John Riegal
Maureen Robinson

Christine Smith
David Smith
Margaret Stedman
Catherine Sutton
Luke Tofts
Mark Tofts
Roy Tofts

Margaret Watts
Doris Watts
Stan Watts

The destination for history
www.thehistorypress.co.uk